# From a Monastery Kitchen

# From a Monastery Kitchen

Elise Boulding

with the assistance of Brother Victor Antonio Avila and Sister Jeanne-Marie Pearse

Illustrations by Daniel Marshall

Harper & Row, Publishers · New York, Hagerstown, San Francisco, London

Grateful acknowledgment is made for permission to reprint art and quotation selections included in this book:

KMTV Omaha for permission to use a photograph which is part of The Bostwick-Frohardt Collection, owned by Station KMTV Omaha, Nebraska. (Page 88, right)

Soeur Sonia, Ste Scholastique, France for photograph which she took. (Pages 60, 61)

D. D. and E. Peter Schroeder, 601 West 115 Street, New York, N.Y. 10025 for photographs. (Pages 8, 9, 10)

The Cloisters located at Fort Tryon Park, New York, N.Y. for its cooperation in the use of the books which make their home in The Cloisters' Library.

The Hogarth Press Ltd for 4 lines from "Field of Autumn" from *The Sun Is My Monument* by Laurie Lee. Reprinted by permission of The Hogarth Press.

Oxford University Press for 5 lines from *The Quarry* by Richard Eberhart. Copyright © 1966 by Richard Eberhart. Reprinted by permission of Oxford Press, Inc.

Rupert Hart-Davis Ltd/Granada Publishing Ltd for 4 lines from "Poetry For Supper" from *Poetry For Supper* (1958) by R. S. Thomas.

Simon & Schuster Inc. for the poems "Hungry Tree" by Nathan Altschuler and "Rain" by Richard Drillich from *Miracles* by Richard Lewis. Copyright © 1966 by Richard Lewis. Reprinted by permission of Simon & Schuster Inc.

National Catholic Rural Life Conference for the Twelfth Night Cake recipe originally appearing in *Cooking For Christ* by Florence Berger. Copyright 1949 by the National Catholic Rural Life Conference, Des Moines, Iowa.

The Liturgical Press for 5 recipes which originally appeared in the following books by Helen McLoughlin: *Family Advent Customs,* (Christollen) page 28; *Christmas To Candlemas In A Catholic Home,* (Arroz Dulce) page 21; *Family Customs: Easter To Pentecost,* (Easter Bread) page 36 and (Pentecost Cake) page 50. Published by the Liturgical Press. Copyrighted by The Order of St. Benedict, Inc. Collegeville, Minnesota.

Library of Congress Cataloging in Publication Data

Boulding, Elise.
    From a monastery kitchen.
    Includes index.
    1. Vegetarian cookery.    2. Monastic and religious life.    I. Title.
TX837.B58      641.5'36      76-9973
ISBN 0-06-060980-X

86    10 9 8 7

# Contents

# Introduction

When our five children were small, some years ago, my morning trip to deliver them to their respective schools took us each day past a local monastery just at the hour when the monks were about in the garden. A few walked with heads bowed; others read their prayer books. The deep silence in the garden somehow penetrated our noisy car, and I never passed that spot without feeling joy.

About two years ago, while seeking a place of quiet retreat between conferences in New York City, I was led to Our Lady of the Resurrection Priory in Cold Spring for a weekend of prayer. Many times since then I have journeyed up the Hudson River on the bumpy Poughkeepsie local to enter the life of prayer that Brother Victor and a novice, Brother Patrick, so generously share with those who come to their farmhouse monastery.

During the first visit I discovered something: monasteries have kitchens, and monks have to cook. I had read about Brother Lawrence, the illiterate lay brother who practiced the presence of God in a monastery kitchen in 17th century Europe in the Middle Ages, but I didn't know that monks continued his practice in twentieth-century kitchens. Not only do monks have to cook, they have to wash dishes and do every kind of housekeeping chore. While they do not usually have young children to feed, they have many guests and must always be ready to set an extra place at the refectory table. As I visited other monasteries, I became more aware of how hard our contemplative brothers and sisters work. Besides household chores, they farm and do craft work and make bread, cheese, or other items to sell. They work as hard as those of us "on the outside" because they too must make ends meet. Monasteries are largely self-supporting.

Since our contemplative brothers and sisters are vowed to a life of poverty, their kitchen work is often hard. Monasteries grow much of their own food, and young monks learn the art of food preservation. There are monks who are gifted cooks, like Brother Victor whose delicious simple meals, served in a spirit of deepest prayer, inspired the idea of this book. At Brother Victor's monastery, this gift for cooking is combined with a gift for frugality that chooses discarded food from supermarket trash bins and lovingly renders society's leavings edible. Brother Victor also has the gift of song, and when he is not in the kitchen, he is sitting at a work table writing and arranging music for the daily hours of prayer (divine office) in the chapel and for the graces sung before meals. Praying, working, cooking, eating, singing, silence, and frugality—all these come together in the sacrament of the refectory.

Many of our monastic brothers and sisters come from farmer stock, like the rest of us, and monastery kitchens reflect the same double feast of body and spirit that the surrounding communities enjoy. Feast days, in fact, probably have always meant more in monasteries than anywhere else because of the sheer contrast with the disciplined asceticism of daily life. A monastic feast day is sober enough at that, but special foods are cooked with such care, special songs sung with such exaltation, that the whole monastery vibrates with holy joy. Holy feasting is not just a safety valve, however; it is a deep reaffirmation of the fact of incarnation. The son of man came eating and drinking.

The cloister *is* very different from the outside world. If it were not, those of us who live in the world would not be drawn there. There is in the monastery a pointing of the whole life toward God, a drawing together of every activity into prayer. Again and again each day the monks return to the chapel, the very heart of every monastery, to lift their hearts to God in silence, in word, and in song throughout the hours bounded by predawn vigils and evening prayers. These two offices, vigils and evening prayer, are like the jeweled gates through which the monks move the world toward heaven every day of their lives.

This book was born in the kitchen of Our Lady of the Resurrection Priory. Having shared the joys of mealtime and even a little

of the weariness of work with my monastic brothers and sisters, it came to me very strongly that this experience should and could be shared with other women and men. This book then is intended to open the monastery door in a symbolic way for those who may never come here but who would like to evoke the peace of the monastery in their own kitchens.

Many people helped to make this book possible. When we decided in Brother Victor's kitchen to do this cookbook, Sister Jeanne Marie Pearse, through correspondence and personal visits to monasteries in North America, France, and Italy, initiated the wonderful flow of recipes. We are grateful to all the brothers and sisters who took the time to sit down and copy out of their own files the recipes we have used here. Since many of the recipes came to us in French, we are particularly grateful to Nancy Gaenslen, who lives in a secular community that serves migrant workers in California, for the long and tedious hours she spent translating the recipes into a form usable in American kitchens. The recipes were not only translated but kitchen-tested in the migrant worker community, which means

that the secular and the monastic world were linked in a very special way during the preparation of the cookbook.

Brother Patrick Francis Shevlin of Our Lady of the Resurrection Priory, and Sister Donald Corcoran, O.S.B., a frequent visitor at the Priory, have shared from the beginning in planning the cookbook. We all shared in the work of finding quotations that would reflect the monastic spirit and its secular counterpart. The final kitchen testing was done by students in two of my classes, adding an unusual dimension to a course in the sociology of religion and a course in the social history of women. Also, students from my conflict and peace studies classes helped find quotations, as did friends among the librarians and teachers of Boulder who share our concerns for simplicity, frugality and peace. Their names are too numerous to mention here, but we are grateful to them and hope they enjoy the book they helped to make! Two very important persons in the actual preparation of the manuscript were Dorothy Carson, my colleague and administrative assistant at the University of Colorado, who organized the assem-

bling of the cookbook, and Judy Fukuhara, who turned recipes scribbled down in every imaginable way into a beautiful usable format.

Finally, we want to express gratitude to Marie Cantlon of Harper & Row, who had the imagination to see what could be done with the original manuscript we brought her, and Marybeth Iskat, her assistant, who spent many hours researching quotations. It has been a great pleasure to work with Dan Marshall, our artist collaborator. He brought great sensitivity as well as his own artistic gifts to the task of translating the monastic vision and the everyday realities of the monastery kitchen into a complete experience for the user of this cookbook.

Elise Boulding
Boulder, Colorado
April 1, 1976

# How to Use This Cookbook

This is a vegetarian cookbook; no meat recipes are included, but there are fish recipes. Not all monastics are vegetarian by any means, but the rule of St. Benedict, which Our Lady of the Resurrection follows, strongly encourages abstaining from meat. And each of us today must consider whether we want more than the least of us on the planet can have; most of our brothers and sisters do not have meat. Frugality takes many forms, and the way of simplicity that is most appropriate for any one household will be unique to that home.

If we were to reconstruct a typical monastic daily fare from the recipes that follow, it might be something like this: Breakfast would be simply coffee and one or two slices of bread (p. 56). Lunch could include lentil and lemon peel soup (p. 91), mixed fruit salad (p. 41), puffed cheese toasts (p. 24), and tea. A supper menu might include vegetable-cheese casserole (p. 65), acorn squash (p. 98), apple crumble (p. 83), and tea.

The dinner table in a monastery is always set with care for both daily fare and feast days. Food is arranged to show the full beauty of God's harvest in vegetables, grains, dairy products, and fruit. Each night before the meal begins, the brothers or sisters of the order stand at their places around the candlelit table and sing grace. Then they quietly settle down to listening to the evening reading from Scripture or a classic religious writing while they eat. The delight in the fellowship of the table is always enhanced by one special ingredient added to every dish served: preparation with love.

The recipes that follow are arranged seasonally in order to link the great rhythms of human life: the seasons of the year, the seasons of the church, and the seasons of the heart. Within each season, recipes are grouped in the order in which they come in the meal, from soup to dessert.

These recipes are in part my record of Brother Victor's preparation of dishes in his monastery kitchen, but they are supplemented by many others that have been sent to us from contemplative monasteries all over the United States, France, and Italy by brothers and sisters who wanted to share a bit of their way of life with householders. Some of them are very simple; some, rather complex. The one thing they have in common is that they are cooked in monastic kitchens. We have tried to avoid recipes that might be found in any standard cookbook. It will be noted that some monasteries have developed a taste for curried dishes in the Indian style!

Each recipe is framed by a collage of quotations and art that is intended to reflect the nearly two-thousand-year-old experience of monastic life as an affirmation of wholeness, simplicity, and joy. Some quotations are directly about monastic life; others represent the same spirit of affirmation from secular life. Other more down-to-earth aids to the user of this book are some cooking hints from one of the sisters who helped prepare this book, four ways to cook fish, and instructions on how to make herbal tea. Many monasteries sell locally the food products they make, such as bread, cheese, and jellies. Contemplative monasteries are strung like rosary beads all across North America, as they also are on every other continent. You may wish to seek out the one nearest you, not only to inquire whether it sells food, but to experience, in the monastery chapel, the grace and joy that is generated in the twentieth-century centers of contemplative life.

# Winter

As soon as the idea of the Deluge
  had subsided.
A hare stopped in the clover
  and swaying flowerbells, and
  said a prayer to the rainbow,
Through the spider's web.

*Arthur Rimbaud, Illuminations*

A leaf swept along by the wind
often looks like a bird.

*Goethe*

Soup and fish explain half of the
emotions of life.

*Sydney Smith*

In my culinary thinking the ingredients are often blended in
my mind, much as a pianist
practices his concert silently,
away from the piano. If you who
read this have never tried mentally to concoct a dish, you may
be surprised to discover you have
the same ability. To experiment,
go where you won't be interrupted
and think of the food you want
to prepare, and what you can do
to improve its flavor and texture.

*Alan Hooker, Vegetarian Gourmet
Cookery*

It it hard for those steeped in the
American culture to understand.
"The fast is a very personal
spiritual thing, and it's not done
out of recklessness," Cesar explains. "It's not done out of a
desire to destroy myself, but it's

---

## Universal European Winter Soup

| | |
|---|---|
| 1 onion | 2 stalks of celery |
| 1 carrot | 1 quart of vegetable stock |
| 1 potato, cut up fine | or add a vegetable |
| | bouillon cube to 1 quart |
| | of water |
| | salt, pepper to taste |

Peel and chop vegetables. Add to vegetable stock.
Bring to boil and simmer for 1 hour.
  Serves 4.

---

done out of a deep conviction
that we can communicate to
people, either those who are for
us or against us, faster and more
effectively spiritually than we
can in any other way."

*Cesar Chavez*

Silence is a privilege to which all
are entitled and of which most
are robbed in this barbaric age.
The monk is not a freak for
loving silence; he is simply nor-
mal and human.

*Matthew Kelty, Aspects of The
Monastic Calling*

---

Lightning can light up the world,
but it can't warm up a stove.

*Friedrich Hebbel*

When icicles hang by the wall,
And Dick the shepherd blows his
  nail,
And Tom bears logs into the hall,
And milk comes frozen home in
  pail,
When blood is nipp'd and ways
  be foul,
Then nightly sings the staring
  owl,
Tu-whit;
Tu-who, a merry note,
While greasy Joan doth keel the
  pot.

When all aloud the wind doth
  blow,
And coughing drowns the par-
  son's saw,
And birds sit brooding in the
  snow,
And Marion's nose looks red
  and raw,
When roasted crabs hiss in the
  bowl,
Then nightly sings the staring
  owl,
Tu-whit;
Tu-who, a merry note,
While greasy Joan doth keel the
  pot.

*William Shakespeare, Winter*

March brings breezes, loud and
   shrill.
To stir the dancing daffodil.
*Mother Goose*

Each day is a little life; every
waking and rising a little birth,
every fresh morning a little youth,
every going to rest and sleep a
little death.
*Arthur Schopenhauer*

Be praised O my Lord by
   Brother Fire
By whom Thou lighteneth our
   steps by night.
For fair is he and merry, master-
   ful and of might.
*St. Francis of Assisi, Canticle of the
Sun*

"The rule is, jam tomorrow, and
jam yesterday—but never jam
today." "It must come sometimes
to 'jam today,'" Alice objected.
"No, it can't," said the Queen.
"It's jam every other day: today
isn't any other day, you know."
*Lewis Carroll, Through the Looking
Glass*

Everything in this world is done
from hope. No farmer would sow
one grain if he did not hope it
would grow to seed. No young

# Potato Soup

| | |
|---|---|
| 3  tablespoons butter | salt, pepper to taste |
| 1  onion, minced very fine |   (1–2 teaspoons sea- |
| 2  quarts milk |   soned salt may be sub- |
| 4  cups mashed potatoes |   stituted) |
| 4  tablespoons flour | 3  tablespoons chopped |
| |    parsley |

Gently sautée onion in butter, without browning, until
softened. Transfer to top of double boiler, over hot
water. Add milk. Stir in potatoes. With wire whip or
baster, beat soup smooth and beat in flour. Add seasoning. Do not boil. When thoroughly hot and smooth,
sprinkle with parsley and serve.
      Serves 8.

man would take a wife, if he
didn't hope to have children by
her. No merchant or working
man would work if he didn't hope
for profit or wages. Then how
much more hope calls us to
eternal life!
*Martin Luther*

When the guest coughs, he wants
a spoon.
*Yiddish Proverb*

Not only do vegetables have
enough water to cook themselves,
most of them also have enough
salt. Approached in the true contemplative spirit—given a chance
to speak for themselves—they
are self-sufficient. There is no
reason for the oceans of brine in
which we usually drown them.
*Father Capon, The Supper of The
Lamb*

For hundreds of thousands of
years, the human race ate its food
raw. But at some time between
the first taming of fire in about
500,000 B.C. and the appearance
of the prehistoric scene of
Neanderthal man, cooking was
discovered. This helped to make
a number of formerly indigestible
foods edible. It also increased
the nutritive value of others,
since heat helps to break down
fibers and release protein and
carbohydrate. The result may
have been improved health and
longer life for developing man.
The distinguished American
anthropologist Carleton Coon
has even suggested that "the in-
troduction of cooking may well
have been the decisive factor in
leading man from a primarily
animal existence into one that
was more fully human."
*Reay Tannahill, Food In History*

A family is a unit composed not
only of children but of men,
women, an occasional animal,
and the common cold.
*Ogden Nash*

Water, taken in moderation, cannot hurt anybody.
*Mark Twain*

Just as eating contrary to the in-
clination is injurious to the
health, so study without desire
spoils the memory, and it retains
nothing that it takes in.
*Leonardo da Vinci*

In growing old, we become more
foolish—and more wise.
*La Rochefoucauld*

Awake, O north wind, and come,
O south wind!
Blow upon my garden, let its
fragrance be wafted abroad.
Let my beloved come to his
garden, and eat its choicest
fruits.
*Song of Solomon 4:16, RSV*

A misty winter, a frosty spring,
a varied summer, and a sunny
harvest [an ideal year].
*Irish Proverb*

Faith. You can do very little
with it, but you can do nothing
without it.
*Samuel Butler*

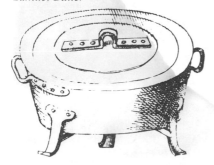

# Chickpea Soup

| | |
|---|---|
| 2 cups chickpeas | 1 stalk celery |
| 3½ cups canned | 2 carrots |
| tomatoes | ½ green pepper |
| 1 large onion | bay leaf, salt, pepper |

Soak chickpeas overnight. Boil, in plenty of water, until soft. Chop vegetables and simmer together with seasonings. Combine with cooked chickpeas and serve as soup.
Serves 8.

All happiness depends on courage and work. I have had many periods of wretchedness, but with energy, and above all, with illusions, I pulled through them all.
*Honoré de Balzac*

Kneel always when you light a
fire!
Kneel reverently and thankful be
For God's unfailing charity.
*John Oxenham, The Sacrament of Fire*

It is only necessary to know that love is a direction and not a state of the soul. If one is unaware of this, one falls into despair at the first onslaught of affliction.
*Simone Weil, Waiting For God*

What makes a fire so pleasant is, I think, that it is a live thing in a dead room.
*Sydney Smith*

They [the Pilgrim Fathers] fell upon an ungenial climate, where there were nine months of winter and three months of cold weather, and that called out the best energies of the men, and of the women too, to get a mere subsistence out of the soil, with such a climate. In their efforts to do that they cultivated industry and frugality at the same time—which is the real foundation of the greatness of the Pilgrims.
*Matthew Arnold, Speech at New England Society Dinner, December 22, 1880*

It is said in an old tale that to understand life man must learn to shudder. This century seems doomed to master the lesson.
*Loren Eiseley*

But the change of mind I am talking about involves not just a change of knowledge, but also a change of attitude toward our essential ignorance, a change in our bearing in the face of mystery. The principle of ecology, if we will take it to heart, should keep us aware that our lives depend upon other lives and upon processes and energies in an interlocking system that, though we can destroy it, we can neither fully understand nor fully control. And our great dangerousness is that, locked in our selfish and myopic economics, we have been willing to change or destroy far beyond our power to understand.
*Wendell Berry, A Continuous Harmony*

Over the land freckled with snow
  half-thawed
The speculating rooks at their
  nests cawed,
And saw from elm-tops, delicate
  as flower of grass,
What we below could not see,
Winter pass.
*Edward Thomas*

There is nothing so wonderful in
any particular landscape as the
necessity of being beautiful under
which every landscape lies.
*Ralph Waldo Emerson*

Nothing is a masterpiece—a real
masterpiece—till it's about two
hundred years old. A picture is
like a tree or a church, you've got
to let it grow into a masterpiece.
Same with a poem or a new religion. They begin as a lot of
funny words. Nobody knows
whether they're all nonsense or a
gift from heaven.
*Joyce Cary*

Cooking is one of those arts
which most require to be done by
persons of a religious nature.
*Alfred North Whitehead*

Friends are a second existence.
*Baltasar Gracián*

The only rational way of educat-
ing is to be an example—if one
can't help it, a warning example.
*Albert Einstein*

# Potato-Red Cabbage Salad
(*Salade de choux rouges*)

½ lb. potatoes
 1 small red cabbage
   *or* 3 or 4 beets
½ cup wine vinegar

2 hard-boiled eggs,
  sliced
  oil and vinegar dress-
  ing

Boil potatoes in jackets, then peel and slice them. Chop
the cabbage, place it in an ovenproof dish, and sprinkle
with vinegar. Bake at 250° for about 20 minutes. Cool.
(Or, boil the beets, slice, sprinkle with vinegar, cool.)
    On a platter, arrange cabbage (or beets) in the
center, potato slices all around. A lovely effect is to
gently separate the yellow egg circles from the whites,
cut each white circle into small pieces and put them
around the yellow to make "daisies" on top of the red
cabbage. (Sprigs of parsley are also a pretty garnish.)
Sprinkle platter with dressing.
    Serves 6.

When we are really honest with
ourselves, we must admit that our
lives are all that really belong to
us. So it is how we use our lives
that determines what kind of
men we are. It is my deepest belief that only by giving our lives
do we find life.
*Cesar Chavez*

Six years you shall sow your field,
and six years you shall prune your
vineyard, and gather in its fruits;
but in the seventh year there shall
be a sabbath of solemn rest for
the land, a sabbath to the Lord;
you shall not sow your field or
prune your vineyard. What grows

of itself in your harvest you shall
not reap, and the grapes of your
undressed vine you shall not
gather; it shall be a year of solemn
rest for the land.
*Leviticus 25:3–5*, RSV

Greatness of soul consists not so
much in soaring high and in pressing forward, as in knowing how
to adapt and limit oneself.
*Montaigne*

**A modest wish: that our doings
and dealings may be of a little
more significance to life than a
man's dinner jacket is to his digestion. Yet not a little of what**

we describe as our achievement
is, in fact, no more than a gar-
ment in which, on festive occa-
sions, we seek to hide our naked-
ness.
*Dag Hammarskjöld, Markings*

The monastic life is by its very
nature "ordinary." Its ordinari-
ness is one of its greatest blessings.
*Thomas Merton*

I believe in getting into hot
water. I think it keeps you clean.
*G. K. Chesterton*

January snowy; February flowy;
  March blowy.
April show'ry; May flow'ry; June
  bow'ry
July moppy, August croppy, September poppy.
October breezy; November
  wheezy; December freezy.
*Richard Brinsley Sheridan*

Burn, wood, burn—
Wood that once was a tree, and
  knew
Blossom and sheaf, and the
Spring's return,
Nest, and singing, and rain, and
  dew—
Burn, wood, burn!
*Nancy Byrd Turner, Flame Song*

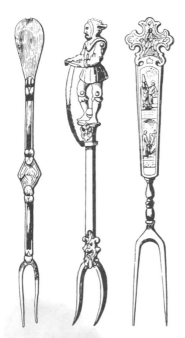

Take long walks in stormy
weather or through deep snow
in the fields and woods, if you
would keep your spirits up. Deal
with brute nature. Be cold and
hungry and weary.
*Henry David Thoreau*

Every people ask: "What can I
actually *do?*" We can, each of

# Dubarry Salad
(*Salade Dubarry*)

| 1 small head cauliflower | 1 cup vinegar |
| 1 quart water | oil and vinegar dressing |

Break cauliflower into very small flowerets. Cover with 1 quart water containing 1 cup vinegar for 15 minutes. Drain thoroughly or dry with towel. Place in bowl with dressing and chill for at least 1 hour.

Serve on a platter surrounded with slices of hard-boiled egg, or tomato, watercress, radishes, etc. Good with mayonnaise.

Serves 4 to 6.

us, work to put our own inner house in order. The guidance we need for this work cannot be found in science or technology, the value of which utterly depends on the ends they serve; but it can still be found in the traditional wisdom of mankind.
*E. F. Schumacher, Small Is Beautiful*

Perhaps the greatest social service that can be rendered by anybody to the country and to mankind is to bring up a family. But here again, because there is nothing to sell, there is a very general disposition to regard a married woman's work as no work at all, and to take it as a matter of course that she should not be paid for it.
*George Bernard Shaw*

Monday's child is fair of face,
Tuesday's child is full of grace,
Wednesday's child is full of woe,
Thursday's child has far to go,
Friday's child is loving and
  giving,
Saturday's child has to work for
  its living,
But a child that's born on the
  Sabbath day
Is fair and wise and good and
  gay.
*Mother Goose*

It is necessary to be almost a genius to make a good husband.
*Honoré de Balzac*

The full stomach makes pure prayer impossible. And the belly stuffed by intemperance prevents attentive psalmody. The sleep of the eater is marred. His dreams are agitated, his visions troubled, his desires frequently excited. This sleep is not healthy rest, but buried under a crushing weight . . . When he rises for psalmody in the night he is not really up. He falls against the wall, he grabs for the posts to support himself; he hangs over the stalls and rests his weight upon them, or rather, suspends upon them the heavy bag full of food which is his body. He is like a dead body among the living. He does not know what psalm is being chanted. He flies into a rage if somebody tries to wake him up. He may even sleep so soundly on his feet that he falls and crashes to the floor, throwing the whole Office into confusion.
*Philoxenus of Mabbog, A.D. 523*

If, after exercise, we feed sparingly, the digestion will be easy and good, the body lightsome, the temper cheerful, and all the animal functions performed agreeably.
*Benjamin Franklin, The Art of Procuring Pleasant Dreams*

For Mercy has a human heart,
Pity a human face,
And Love, the human form
  divine,
And Peace, the human dress.

And all must love the human
  form,
In heathen, Turk, or Jew;
Where Mercy, Love, and Pity
  dwell
There God is dwelling too.

*William Blake*

Jesus' "lack of moral principles."
He sat at meat with publicans
and sinners, he consorted with
harlots. Did he do this to obtain
their votes? Or did he think that,
perhaps, he could convert them
by such "appeasement"? Or was
his humanity rich and deep
enough to make contact, even in

# Mixed Vegetable Curry

| | | | |
|---|---|---|---|
| 1 | lb. green peas | 4 | tablespoons butter |
| ¾ | lb. carrots | 3 | onions, sliced thin |
| 1⅓ | lbs. potatoes | 2 | teaspoons chopped mint leaves |
| 1 | lb. string beans | | |
| 1 | clove garlic | ½ | cup yogurt |
| ¾ | tablespoon green ginger (¼ teaspoon powdered) | ¾ | tablespoon cumin |
| | | 1½ | tablespoons tomato paste |
| 2 | tablespoons turmeric (optional) | ½ | teaspoon black pepper, salt to taste |

Shell and wash peas. Peel and dice carrots. Peel and halve the potatoes, add beans. Mix them together in a casserole or saucepan of boiling water. Cover, remove from heat, and reserve.

Pound the garlic and ginger (and turmeric, if desired) and mix with ¾ cup water. Melt the butter and fry the onions. When onions are well browned, add the chopped mint leaves. Fry for a minute more, then add the yogurt and cumin. Cook very gently for 5 minutes. Add the vegetables, drained. Cook for another 10 minutes. Then add the ginger-garlic water, with tomato paste, pepper, and salt. Cook until the liquid is dry. Now add 2 cups of the water from the vegetables. Cook covered (adding more water if necessary) until done.

Serves 8.

them, with that in human nature which is common to all men, indestructible, and upon which the future has to be built?

*Dag Hammarskjöld, Markings*

It's a lot worse to be soul-hungry than to be body-hungry.

*A Kentucky mountain woman asking for her granddaughter to be admitted to Berea College high school [c. 1900] Quoted by Carl R. Woodward in The Wonderful World of Books*

Such is life. It is no cleaner than a kitchen; it reeks of a kitchen; and if you mean to cook your dinner, you must expect to soil your hands; the real art is getting them clean again, and therein lies the whole morality of our epoch.

*Honoré de Balzac*

It is not by driving away our brother than we can be alone with God.

*George Macdonald*

And the light shone in darkness and
Against the World the unstilled world still whirled
Above the centre of the silent Word.
*T. S. Eliot, Ash Wednesday*

For everything there is a season, and a time for every matter under heaven. . . .
A time to be born . . .
A time to plant . . .
A time to uproot what has been planted . . .
A time to be silent . . .
A time to love . . .
*Ecclesiastes 3:2, 7, 8,* RSV

Solitude is the dwelling place of the saints and silence is their language.
*Author Unknown*

# Parsley-Potato Casserole

3 cloves garlic, chopped
3 tablespoons of oil
8 potatoes, peeled and sliced

1 large onion, chopped
½ cup chopped parsley
salt, pepper

Briefly sauté chopped garlic in oil. Butter a two-quart casserole dish. Fill with layers as follows: sliced potatoes, chopped onions, chopped garlic, a liberal sprinkling of parsley, salt, and pepper. Repeat layers. Dot top with butter, salt, and pepper. Along edge (so as not to wash off seasonings), pour in water about ⅔ to ¾ full (do not cover potatoes entirely). Cover the casserole. Bake at 350° for 1½ hours, removing cover for last twenty minutes.
   Serves 6 to 8.

If modern civilized man had to kill the animals he eats, the number of vegetarians would rise astronomically.
*Christian Morgenstern*

To mankind in general Macbeth and Lady Macbeth stand out as the supreme type of all that a host and hostess should not be.
*Max Beerbohm*

God does not die on the day when we cease to believe in a personal deity, but we die on the day when our lives cease to be illuminated by the steady radiance, renewed daily, of a wonder, the source of which is beyond all reason.
*Dag Hammarskjöld, Markings*

There is no pot so ugly that a cover cannot be found for it.
*English Proverb*

Nature loves to hide.
*Heraclitus*

I was born and bred in the country and among field-laborers; I have had the business of husbandry in my own hands ever since my predecessors of the property I enjoy left me to succeed in it. And yet I can add up neither with counters nor with a pen. Most of our coins are unknown to me. I cannot differentiate between one grain and another, either in the ground or in the barn, unless the difference be too glaring; and can scarcely distinguish between the cabbages and lettuces in my garden. I do not even know the names of the chief implements of husbandry, nor the rude principles of agriculture, which the boys know. I know still less of the mechanical arts, of trade and merchandise, of the nature and diversity of fruits, wines, and foodstuffs, of training a hawk or physicking a horse or a hound. And, to complete my disgrace, only a month ago I was caught in ignorance of the fact that leaven is used in making bread, and of the meaning of allowing wine to ferment.
*Montaigne*

A change in the weather is enough to renew the world and ourselves.
*Marcel Proust*

I give you for the month of
   January
Courtyards and hall where fires
   flame and flare.
*Folgore da San Gimignano, 1305,*
*Seasons*


Horses, Dogs, Haulkes, Servants,
Superbe Pallaces, long Tables,
doe vndoe the greatest Lords,
and make them shortly miserable.

*English Proverb, 16th Century*

# Benedictine Orange Rice

¼ cup butter, mar-
   garine, or cooking oil
½ cup chopped celery
½ cup chopped onion
1 cup uncooked rice,
   brown or white
1⅓ cups orange juice
   plus enough water to
   make amount re-
   quired by rice you
are using (see pack-
   age directions)
1 vegetable bouillon
   cube
1 tablespoon grated
   orange rind
1 teaspoon salt
½ cup raisins
   (optional)

Melt butter or margarine in saucepan or baking dish.
Add celery and onions and sauté until tender. Add rice
and sauté until all grains are coated with oil and golden
brown. Add orange juice and water and bring to a boil.
Stir in orange peel, salt, and raisins. Cover pan with
tight lid or foil. Bake at 350° for about 30 minutes for
white rice, 1 hour for brown. This can also be simmered
on very low heat on top of the stove.
   Serves 6.

Love, and do what you like.
*St. Augustine*


In a slumber visional,
Wonders apparitional
Sudden shone on me:
Was it not a miracle?
Built of lard coracle
Swam a sweet milk sea.

With high hearts heroical
We stepped in it, stoical
Braving billow-bounds;
Then we rode so dashingly,
Smote the sea so splashingly,
That the surge sent, washingly,
Honey up for grounds.

Ramparts rose of custard all
Where a castle muster'd all
Forces o'er the lake;
Butter was the bridge of it,
Wheaten meal the ridge of it,
Bacon every stake.

Strong it stood and pleasantly
There I entered presently
Hying to the hosts;
Dry beef was the door of it,
Bare bread was the floor of it,
Whey-curls were the posts.

Old cheese-columns happily,
Pork that pillard sappily,
Raised their heads aloof;
While curd-rafters mellowly

Crossing cream-beams yellowly,
Held aloft the roof.

Wine in well rose sparkingly,
Beer was rolling darkingly,
Bragget brimmed the pond.
Lard was oozing heavily,
Merry malt moved wavily,
Through the floor beyond.

Lake of broth lay spicily
Fat froze o'er it icily,
'Tween the wall and shore;
Butter rose in hedges high,
Cloaking all its edges high.

White lard blossomed o'er
Apple alleys bowering,
Pink-topped orchards flowering
Fenced off hill and wind;
Leek-tree forests loftily,
Carrots branching tuftily,
Guarded it behind.

Ruddy warders rosily
Welcomed us right cosily
To the fire and rest;
Seven coils of sausages,
Twined in twisted passages,
Round each brawny breast.

Their chief I discover him,
Suet mantle over him,
By his lady bland;
Where the cauldron boiled away,
The Dispenser toiled away,
With his fork in hand.

Good King Cathal, royally,
Surely will enjoy a lay,
Fair and fine as silk;
From his heart his woe I call,
When I sing, heroical,
How we rode, so stoical,
O'er the Sea of Milk.
*The Portable Medieval Reader, James*
*Bruce Ross & Mary Martin McLaugh-*
*lin, eds. "Bards of the Gael and Gall"*


If we would not share the little
   we have,
We would not give although we
   had everything at our command.
*William Blake*

Sometimes hath the brightest
   day a cloud
And after summer evermore
   succeeds
Barren winter, with his wrathful
   nipping cold:
So cares and joys abound, as
   seasons fleet.
*Shakespeare, King Henry VI*

There is one spectacle grander
   than the sea,
That is the sky;
There is one spectacle grander
   than the sky,
That is the interior of the soul.
*Victor Hugo*

Be ready at all times for the
gifts of God and always for new
ones.
*Meister Eckhart*

# Beans Bengal

| | |
|---|---|
| 1 lb. dried yellow split peas or baby lima beans | ½ cup minced onion |
| | ½ cup minced green pepper |
| ½ lb. sharp cheddar cheese, broken up or grated | ¼ cup olive or salad oil |
| | ¾ cup seedless raisins |
| 3 teaspoons curry powder | salt |

Soak the beans overnight in cold water, drain, and par-boil in fresh water (with 1 teaspoon salt) for 1 hour or until semisoft. Combine the beans with all other in-gredients, leaving enough of the water peas were cooked in to keep the casserole moist. Add salt. Mix well and put into a baking pan or dish. Bake at 300° for 2 hours. Stir occasionally, and add enough bean water while baking to keep the beans moist but not runny. Serve hot.

When the dish is prepared in the above way, the cheese melts completely and becomes invisible. If you prefer to have the chunks melt but remain intact, add the cheese during the last 15 minutes of baking time.

This dish can also be adapted as a cold salad. Cook the beans in water until they are completely done. Drain and mix with all other ingredients (plump the raisins in water first), increasing the oil and adding a little vine-gar until the ingredients are coated lightly. Chill and serve.

Serves 6 to 8.

The dynamic principle of fantasy is play, which belongs also to the child, and as such it appears to be inconsistent with the principle of serious work. But without this playing with fantasy no creative work has ever yet come to birth. The debt we own to the play of imagination is incalculable.
*Carl Jung*

Children think not of what is past, nor what is to come, but enjoy the present time, which few of us do.
*Jean de La Bruyère*

It is always the secure who are humble.
*G. K. Chesterton*

If Candlemas Day be fair and
bright,
Winter will have another flight;
But if it be dark with clouds and
rain,
Winter is gone, and will not come
again.
*Mother Goose*

Nature does nothing in vain.
*Sir Thomas Browne, Religio Medici*

Uphold us, cherish, and have
power to make
Our noisy years seem moments
in the being
Of the Eternal Silence: truths
that wake
To perish never.
*William Wordsworth, (Ode)
Intimations of Immortality From
Recollections of Early Childhood*

# Italian-Style Fish Fillets

(*Tranches à l'italienne*)

| | | | |
|---|---|---|---|
| 1½ | cups tomato sauce | 1 | egg, slightly beaten |
| 2 | tablespoons butter | ½ | cup flour |
| 3 | tablespoons oil | | olives, parsley sprigs |
| 4 | slices filleted fish | | for garnish |
| | | | salt and pepper |

Prepare a good tomato sauce; have it hot in a saucepan.
Melt butter and oil in a heavy frying pan. Dip the fish
in egg, then in flour. Season. Fry gently for a total of
10 to 15 minutes, depending on thickness.

Arrange fish on platter, garnish; spoon a little of
the sauce on them, and serve the rest of the sauce in a
gravy boat.

Serves 4.

Hospitality consists in a little fire,
a little food, and an immense
quiet.
*Ralph Waldo Emerson*

A man's own dinner is to himself
so important that he cannot bring
himself to believe that it is a matter utterly indifferent to anyone
else.
*Anthony Trollope*

A meal, however simple, is a
moment of intersection. It is at
once the most basic, the most
fundamental, of our life's activities, maintaining the life of our
bodies; shared with others it can

be an occasion of joy and communion, uniting people deeply.
*Elise Boulding*

If you would have guests merry
with cheer, be so yourself, or so
at least appear.
*Benjamin Franklin*

He remains a fool his whole life
long
Who loves not women, wine, and
song.
*Martin Luther*

Nothing has a stronger influence
psychologically on their environment, and especially on their
children, than the unlived life of
the parents.
*C. G. Jung*

If we could learn how to utilize
all the intelligence and patent
good will children are born with,
instead of ignoring much of it—
why—*there might be enough to
go around!*
*Dorothy Canfield Fisher*

The telescope makes the world
smaller; it is only the microscope
that makes it larger.
*G. K. Chesterton*

And God's sheer daylight
Pours through our shafted sky
To proffer again
The still occasion of His grace
Where we might meet each other.
*Brother Antoninus, Hospice of the
Word*

This is about the stillness in
    moving things,
In running water, also in the
    sleep
Of winter seeds, where time to
    come has tensed
Itself, enciphering a script so fine
Only the hourglass can magnify
    it, only
The years unfold its sentence
    from the root.
*Howard Nemorov, Runes*

In the fourteenth century, as in
most other eras, the poor man's
meal was in a class by itself. It
still consisted of dark bread made
from rye, barley, or maslin—
sometimes with pea or bean flour
mixed in—and a *companaticum*
from the stockpot, with some
cheese perhaps, or a bowl of
curds to round the meal off. Ser-

# Brother Victor's Lentil Soufflé

1 cup thick white sauce
 (3 tablespoons butter,
 3 tablespoons flour, 1
 cup milk, ¼ teaspoon
 salt, dash nutmeg, and
 pepper)

3 eggs separated, whites
 beaten stiff
1 cup grated cheddar
 cheese
1 cup cooked lentils
1 onion, chopped fine

Make white sauce. Add egg yolks while stirring. Add
cheese, stir until melted. Add lentils and chopped
onions. Add beaten egg whites. Place in greased two-
quart oven dish, and bake at 450° for 20 minutes;
finish baking at 350° about another 25 minutes.
    Serves 6.

vants in large country households
were better fed than the peasant
in his hut. Sometimes they might
have beef or goose, as well as
maslin bread, pease pudding,
salt herring, dried cod, cheese,
and ale brewed on the estate.
*Reay Tannahill, Food In History*

Small rooms or dwellings set the
mind in the right path, large ones
cause it to go astray.
*Leonardo da Vinci*

Some people use other than
physical food to assuage their
hunger—money, sex, social

status, etc., but still the simplest
comfort is palatable food. There
may be such a thing as going
beyond this eternal sense of hunger to another level of our being
which does not hunger, but this
journey is not taken by many
people.
*Alan Hooker, Vegetarian Gourmet
Cookery*

You are the salt of the earth.
*Matthew 5:13,* RSV

When an apprentice gets hurt, or
complains of being tired, the
workmen and peasants have this
fine expression: "It is the trade

entering his body." Each time
that we have some pain to go
through, we can say to ourselves
quite truly that it is the universe,
the order, and beauty of the
world and the obedience of creation of God that are entering our
body.
*Simone Weil, Waiting For God*

The Christian life is a journey . . .
Therefore do not wait for great
strength before setting out, for
immobility will weaken you
further. Do not wait to see very
clearly before starting: one has
to walk toward the light.
*The Choice Is Always Ours, Dorothy
Berkley Phillips, ed.*

So I found
That hunger was a way
Of persons outside windows,
The entering takes away.
*Emily Dickinson*

We cannot become saints merely
by trying to run away from material things.
*Thomas Merton*

For prayer and psalmody every
hour is suitable, that while one's
hands are busy with their tasks
we may praise God with the
tongue, or, if not, with the heart.
*St. Basil*

When my spirit soars, my body
falls on its knees.
*G. C. Lichtenberg*

Many's the long night I dreamed of cheese—toasted, mostly.
*Robert Louis Stevenson*

Daffodils that come before the swallow does
And take the winds of March with beauty.
*Spenser, Faerie Queene*

Great men, like nature, use simple language.
*Vauvenargues*

At the moment of birth a problem is created which has to be faced every day as long as one lives. That problem is one's relationship to the environment. The infant solves the problem by feeding and thus conditions

# Puffed Cheese Toasts

| 6 slices whole wheat bread | salt, pepper |
| 2 eggs | ¾ cup grated Swiss cheese |

Toast bread lightly. Beat eggs. Beat in seasonings and cheese to make a very stiff paste. (You may vary amount of cheese.) Spread paste on toast slices. Place under broiler for 3 to 5 minutes or until golden brown and puffed up.

Serve immediately. (Paste can be made ahead of time, kept cold, then spread and cooked at last minute.)

Serves 6.

himself from the beginning with the idea that when one is in trouble—or in a strange situation—and can think of nothing else to do, one eats. In one form or another this idea haunts us all the days of our lives.
*Alan Hooker, Vegetarian Gourmet Cookery*

It would seem to the unthinking that mothers of children, whether of one or of a dozen, are intensely preoccupied with creatures: their little ones, food, clothing, shelter, matters that are down to earth and grossly material such as dirty diapers, dishes, cooking, cramming baby mouth's with food, etc. Womens' bodies, heavy with children, dragged down by children, are a weight like a cross to be carried about. From morning until night they are preoccupied with care for others, for the duties God has given them. It is a road once set out upon, from which there is no turning back.
*Dorothy Day*

There will be time, there will be time
To prepare a face to meet the faces that you meet;
And time yet for a hundred indecisions,

And for a hundred visions and revisions,
Before the taking of a toast and tea.
*T. S. Eliot, The Wasteland*

Whoever loves much, does much.
*Thomas a Kempis*

Why are we by all creatures waited on?
Why do the prodigal elements supply
Life and food to me, being more pure than I,
Simple, and further from corruption?
*John Donne*

May blessings light upon him who first invented sleep! It is food for the hungry, drink for the thirsty, heat for the cold, and cold for the hot. It is the coin that buys all things, and the balance that makes the king even with the shepherd, and the fool with the wise.
*Cervantes*

Happy the man, whose wish and
care
A few paternal acres bound,
Content to breathe his native air
In his own ground.
Whose herds with milk, whose
fields with bread,
Whose flocks supply him with at-
tire;
Whose trees in summer yield him
shade,
In winter, fire.
*Alexander Pope*

I drink, I eat, array myself, and
live.
*William Shakespeare, Merry Wives of
Windsor*

The strongest animals in the
jungles are not man-eaters. They
and vegetarians and fruitarians.
They don't need meat to make
them strong! What are the strongest animals in the jungle? The
lion—the "king of the jungle"?
No. The tiger? No. The giant of
the jungle, of course, is the elephant. And what does the elephant eat? Fruit, leaves and
young branches. Unless the
elephant is in a zoo, where
peanuts may become a substitute
for a jungle diet. The elephant is
a vegetarian.
*Dick Gregory, Dick Gregory's Natural
Diet for Folks Who Eat: Cookin' with
Mother Nature*

# Old-fashioned Potato Pancakes
(*Crique à l'ancienne*)

| | |
|---|---|
| 5 or 6 medium potatoes | 1 tablespoon fresh |
| 6 eggs | parsley, chopped |
| ⅓ cup milk | salt, pepper to taste |
| 3 tablespoons fresh | butter for frying |
| onion, grated | |

Grate the potatoes coarsely. Beat the eggs slightly and
stir in the milk, potatoes, onion, and parsley. Season
to taste with salt and pepper. Be generous with the
butter when frying (delicious as well as prevents sticking). Drop potato mixture by spoonfuls into melted
butter in pan. Cover and cook 10 minutes over moderate heat. It helps to dot a little butter on the top so that
when the pancakes are turned over the other side
browns without sticking. Fry the second side about 5
minutes.
     Serves 6.

To learn that one is not particularly bright, not uncommonly
gifted with imagination, unwise,
wild, not very kind, impatient,
easily bored, rather blind, not
especially sensitive, unworthy of
prolonged attention—to learn
these things about oneself is to be
at a great advantage in terms of
humility. Great pride is then possible.
*John Berry*

To be sure, our mental processes
often go wrong, so that we imagine God to have gone away. What
should be done then? Do exactly
what you would do if you felt

most secure. Learn to behave
thus even in deepest distress and
keep yourself that way in any and
every estate of life. I can give you
no better advice than to find God
where you lost him.
*Meister Eckhart*

Get me some repast; I care not
what, so it be wholesome food.
*William Shakespeare, Taming of the
Shrew*

Perhaps the efforts of the true
poets, founders, religious, litera-
tures, all ages, have been, and
ever will be, our time and times
to come, essentially the same—to

bring people back from their
present strayings and sickly ab-
stractions, to the costless, aver-
age, divine, original concrete.
*Walt Whitman*

During the early Middle Ages
the monasteries helped preserve
the best of Roman gastronomy
as well as other aspects of the
old culture. Along with other
manuscripts, the churchmen
saved recipes. And because their
food supplies were meager—as
a consequence of both the un-
certain times and the asceticism
of early Christianity—the monks
learned to cook even the meanest
of vegetables (such as the turnip)
so that they tasted good.
*Waverley Root, The Cooking of Italy*

Hee that will not labour in
haruest, must begge in winter.
*English Proverb, 16th Century*

Lift up your heart to Him, sometimes even at your meals, and
when you are in company; the
least little remembrance will always be acceptable to Him. You
need not cry very loud; He is
nearer to us than we are aware of.
*Brother Lawrence*

Humor is the contemplation of
the finite from the point of view
of the infinite.
*Christian Morgenstern*

Hope is a good breakfast, but it
is a bad supper.
*Francis Bacon, De Augmentis
Scientiarum*

Hunger is the best cook.
*Ginzberger, Der Zuchts Spiegel, 1610*

It is a beauteous evening, and
   free,
The holy time is quiet as a Nun
Breathless with adoration: the
   broad sun
Is sinking down in its tranquillity;
The gentleness of heaven broods
   o'er the Sea:
Listen! the mighty Being is
   awake,
And doth with his eternal motion
   make
A sound like thunder—everlast-
   ing.

*William Wordsworth*

Would it be too bold to imagine,
that in the great length of time,
since the earth began to exist,
perhaps millions of ages before
the commencement of the history
of mankind, would it be too bold
to imagine, that all warm-
blooded animals have arisen
from one living filament which
the Great First Cause endued
with animality . . . and thus pos-
sessing the faculty of continuing
to improve by its own inherent
activity, and of delivering down

# Oatmeal Croquettes

(*Croquettes de flocons d'avoine*)

| | |
|---|---|
| 4 eggs, separated | oil for cooking |
| 1 medium onion, chopped fine | 3–4 tomatoes, cut in chunks |
| 2 tablespoons chopped parsley | parsley, thyme, basil, bay leaf |
| 1¼ cup grated Swiss cheese | 1 clove garlic, chopped fine |
| 1 cup dry oatmeal flour to coat croquettes | salt and pepper |

Beat egg whites until stiff. Combine egg yolks, onion,
parsley, grated cheese. Beat well; beat in egg whites
and gradually add the oatmeal. Form into 1-inch balls
(if mixture is not firm enough, add more oats). Roll in
flour. Heat oil in heavy pot. Brown croquettes on all
sides. Drain off any excess oil. Combine tomatoes,
herbs, garlic, seasonings. Pour into pot. Cover and cook
over moderate heat about 20 minutes.
   Serves 4.

those improvements by generation to its posterity, world without end!

*Erasmus Darwin, Zoonomia*

Mysticism, the hyphen between
paganism and Christianity.

*Charles Baudelaire*

Concern for the future is the
mark and glory of the human
condition. Men come and go,
but however limited their individual strength, small their con-
tribution, and short their life
span, their efforts are never in
vain because like runners in a
race, they hand on the torch of
life.

*René Dubos*

Afraid! Of whom am I afraid?
Not Death—for who is He?
The Porter of my Father's
   Lodge
As much abasheth me!

*Emily Dickinson*

Can a sparrow know how a stork
feels?

*Goethe*

Let us eat and drink, for tomorrow we die.

*Isaiah 22:13, RSV*

Heap high the farmer's wintry
  hoard!
Heap high the golden corn!
No richer gift has Autumn poured
From out her lavish horn!
*John Greenleaf Whittier*

Live within your harvest.
*Persian Proverb*

Man is a very comic creature,
and most of the things he does
are comic—eating, for instance.
And the most comic things of all
are exactly the things that are
most worth doing—such as making love.
*G. K. Chesterton*

At the beginning of a marriage
ask yourself whether this woman
will be interesting to talk to from
now until old age. Everything else
in marriage is transitory: most of
the time is spent in conversation.
*Friedrich Nietzsche*

Love consists in this that two
solitudes protect and touch and
greet each other.
*Rainer Maria Rilke*

# Corn Meal Mush

(*Polenta*)

| | |
|---|---|
| 1 cup cold water | 4 tablespoons olive oil |
| 1 cup yellow corn meal | ¾ teaspoon salt |
| 1 teaspoon salt | 1 1-lb. can tomatoes |
| 3 cups boiling water | 1 6-oz. can tomato paste |
| 1 cup chopped onion | ½ teaspoon oregano |
| 2 cloves garlic, crushed |   dash of pepper to taste |
| 2 green peppers, well chopped | 1 cup grated yellow cheese |

Combine cold water, corn meal, and salt. Pour into the
boiling water, stirring very well. Bring to a boil, stirring
constantly. Reduce heat, cover the pot. Let it cook for
5 minutes, stirring occasionally. Pour into a big greased
ovenproof dish.

    *Sauce:* Sauté onion, garlic, and green peppers in
the olive oil. Add salt, tomatoes, tomato paste, oregano,
and dash of pepper. Boil, stirring frequently. Reduce
heat and simmer for ½ hour. Pour the sauce over the
polenta and spread grated cheese over it. Bake for
about 15 to 20 minutes in a 350° oven.

    Makes 8 servings.

In many homes the evening is
the only time when the busy
father has the opportunity, and
the mother the leisure, to share
in the pursuits and pasttimes of
the children. If children do not
find pleasure and entertainment
at home they will seek it elsewhere, often in undesirable directions. Hence every parent should
strive to make children feel that
home is the happiest place in the
world.
*Mrs. Beeton's Household Management*

If there is anything that we wish
to change in the child, we should
first examine it and see whether
it is not something that could
better be changed in ourselves.
*Carl Jung*

An error is the more dangerous
in proportion to the degree of
truth which is contains.
*Frédéric Amiel*

You are my God. Teach me to do
your will.
*St. Francis of Assisi*

A crust eaten in peace is better
than a banquet partaken in
anxiety.
*Aesop, The Town Mouse and the
Country Mouse*

The spider expects the cold of
    winter.
When the shadows fall in long
    Autumn
He congeals in a nest of paper,
    prepares
The least and minimal existence,
Obedient to nature. No other
    course
Is his; no other availed him when
In high summer he spun and
    furled
The gaudy catches. I am that
    spider
Caught in nature, summer and
    winter.

*Richard Eberhart*


He who is joined with all the living has hope.

*Ecclesiastes 9:4, RSV*


For ye shall go out in joy, and be
    led forth in peace;
The mountains and the hills be-
    fore you shall break forth into
    singing,
And all the trees of the field shall
    clap their hands.

*Isiah 55:12, RSV*

# Butterscotch Pudding

(*Crème meunière au caramel*)

| | |
|---|---|
| 2 cups milk | 4 tablespoons flour |
| 1 cup caramel candy squares | whipped cream (optional) |
| 4 tablespoons butter | |

Heat milk and caramels together until candy melts.
Melt butter. Stir in flour and let cook, stirring frequently
and without browning the butter, for about 5 minutes.
Stir milk and caramel mixture into butter mixture;
bring to boil, stirring. Chill thoroughly. Serve with
whipped cream on top if desired.

Serves 5.

The merry, but unlook'd for
    guest,
Full often proves to be the best.

*William Combe, Dr. Syntax's Tour in
Search of Consolation*


What is there in the vale of life
Half so delightful as a wife,
When friendship, love, and peace
    combine
To stamp the marriage bond di-
    vine?

*William Cowper*


Teacher, tender comrade, wife,
A fellow-farer true through life,
Heart-whole and soul-free,

The august Father gave to me.

*Robert Louis Stevenson*


The wife is the key of the house.

*Thomas Fuller, Gnomologia*


Father, help us to live as the Holy
Family united in respect and love.
Bring us to the joy and peace of
your eternal home. Through
Christ our Lord. Amen.

*From the Roman Missal*


The shepherd for food follows
not the sheep.

*William Shakespeare, Two Gentlemen
of Verona*

Hunger does not breed reform; it
breeds madness and all ugly dis-
tempers that make an ordered life
impossible.

*Woodrow Wilson*

St. Bonaventure said that after
the long fast of our Lord in the
desert, when the angels came to
minister to Him, they went first
to the Blessed Mother to see what
she had on her stove, and got the
soup she had prepared and trans-
ported it to our Lord, who rel-
ished it the more because His
Mother had prepared it. Of
course.

*Dorothy Day*


The happiest life, seen in perspective, can hardly be better than a
stringing together of odd little
moments.

*Norman Douglas*


God bless the Ground! I shall
    walk softly there,
And learn by going where I have
    to go.

*Theodore Roethke, The Waking*

There is a pleasure in the path-
  less woods,
There is a rapture on the lonely
  shore,
There is society where none in-
  trudes
By the deep sea, and music in its
  roar:
I love not man the less, but nature more,
From these our interviews, in
  which I steal
From all I may be, or have been
  before,
To mingle with the universe, and
  feel
What I can ne'er express, yet
  cannot all conceal.

*Lord Byron, The Sea*

Speech is the organ of this present
  world,
Silence is the mystery of the
  world to come.

*Isaac of Ninive*

If the day is fine, any walk will
do; it all looks good.

*Annie Dillard, Pilgrim at Tinker Creek*

Instinctively, obstinately, the con-
templative searches for the Stable
One, the Unchanging One, the
Absolute One.

*Pierre Teilhard de Chardin*

Belief is better than anything else,
and it is best when rapt, above
paying its respects to anybody's

# Charterhouse Pudding

(*Gâteau chartrain*)

| | |
|---|---|
| 1 6-oz. package chocolate bits (or 6 oz. milk chocolate or bittersweet chocolate, or 3 oz. unsweetened chocolate) | 3 cups milk |
| | 2 tablespoons instant tapioca |
| | ¼ cup farina |
| | 1 teaspoon vanilla whipped cream (optional) |
| ⅓ cup sugar | |

Melt the chocolate in the milk with the sugar; bring just
to boiling point. Sprinkle in tapioca and farina; cook
10 minutes, stirring frequently, until pudding is thickened. Add vanilla. Chill thoroughly, serve with whipped
cream topping. This pudding is excellent for molds.
  Serves 6.

doubts whatsoever.
*Robert Frost*

Painting is the intermediate somewhat between a thought and a
thing.
*Sydney Smith*

You can think as much as you
like but you will invent nothing
better than bread and salt.
*Russian Proverb*

To be without a sense of taste is
to be deficient in an exquisite
faculty, that of appreciating the
qualities of food, just as a person
may lack the faculty of appreciat

ing the quality of a book or a
work of art. It is to want a vital
sense, one of the elements of
human superiority.
*Guy de Maupassant*

Taste cannot be controlled by
law.
*Thomas Jefferson*

Economy is the art of making the
most of life. The love of economy
is the root of all virtue.
*George Bernard Shaw*

Fasting is a medicine.
*St. John Chrysostom*

The world of the living contains
enough marvels and mysteries
acting upon our emotions and intelligence in ways so inexplicable
that it would almost justify the
conception of life as an enchanted
state.
*Joseph Conrad*

God gave a Loaf to every Bird
But just a Crumb—to Me.
*Emily Dickinson*

The bird of wisdom flies low, and
seeks her food under hedges.
*Walter Savage Landor*

Appetite comes with eating . . .
but the thirst goes away with
drinking.
*François Rabelais*

And when mealtime came, St.
Francis and St. Clare sat down
together, and first one of the
companions of St. Francis with
the companion of St. Clare, then
all of the other brothers, humbly
gathered around the table. As
they began to eat, St. Francis
began to speak of God so gently
and profoundly and marvelously
that divine grace descended upon
them in such abundance that they
were all lifted up to God. And
they remained enraptured, with
their eyes and hands raised up
to God.

At that same time the men of
Assisi and Bettona and the sur-
ounding towns saw St. Mary of
the Angels, the surrounding land,
and the forest all aflame, and
they ran down with great haste
to extinguish the flames. But
when they came to the place, they
found nothing on fire. They
entered and found St. Francis
with St. Clare and all the brothers

# Dessert Pancakes

(*Crêpes*)

| | | |
|---|---|---|
| 3 | eggs (for tenderer crêpes, use only the yolks) | |
| 1½ | cups sifted flour | |
| 1 | cup milk | |
| ½ | cup water | |
| 4 | tablespoons melted butter | |

| | |
|---|---|
| 2 | tablespoons orange liqueur |
| 1 | tablespoon sugar |
| 2 | tablespoons grated orange rind |
| | powered sugar (superfine, not confectioners) |

Beat eggs. Beat flour in gradually, then milk, water, and
melted butter. Dough must "rest," covered and in refrigerator, at least 2 hours; overnight is good. Stir in
orange liqueur, sugar, grated orange rind. Use a small
frying pan, preferably one with low sides, no more than
7 inches in diameter. Oil or butter it for each crêpe.
Pour about 3 tablespoons of batter into warm pan and
rotate to spread batter evenly over surface. Batter
should be very thin. (Trial and error will lead to best
heat to use, whether to add a few tablespoons of milk
to thin batter slightly, etc.) When one side is brown,
run spatula around edge of crêpe, then under it, and
turn it to brown other side. As each crêpe is done,
sprinkle powdered sugar on surface and fold in quarters. Stack and cover with sheet of waxed paper.

Serves 4, about 12 crêpes.

seated around that humble table,
rapt in the contemplation of God.
They understood then that the
fire was a divine and miraculous
fire, a sign of the divine love
burning within the souls of those
holy brothers and sisters. And
they returned to their towns comforted in their hearts and edified.

Later, a long while after, St.
Francis and St. Clare and all the
others came to themselves, so
well comforted with spiritual
nourishment that they had little
concern for bodily food. And
when that blessed meal was over,
St. Clare, well accompanied, returned to St. Damian's.
*How St. Clare Ate a Meal with St.
Francis and His Friars, The Little
Flowers of St. Francis of Assisi*

I wish to astonish Paris with an apple.
*Paul Cézanne*

The pure taste of the apple is as much a contact with the beauty of the universe as the contemplation of a picture by Cézanne. And more people are capable of savouring a compote of apple than of contemplating Cézanne.
*Simone Weil*

## Molasses Apple Cake

1½ cups thinly sliced apples
¾ cup molasses
⅓ cup shortening
½ cup hot water
2½ cups flour
½ cup sugar

1 teaspoon cinnamon
½ teaspoon cloves
¼ teaspoon nutmeg
1 tablespoon baking powder
¼ teaspoon salt

Slowly cook apples in molasses until tender. Cool. Melt shortening in hot water. Sift all dry ingredients, and gradually add the hot water mixture, stirring constantly to keep smooth. Stir in molasses and apple mixture. Pour into greased oblong 8 by 12–inch pan. Bake at 350° for about 30 minutes. Serve warm.

at the same time calling for different things, I possess God in as great tranquility as if I were upon my knees at the blessed sacrament."
*Brother Lawrence*

Here's to thee, old apple tree,
Here's to thee, old apple tree!
Well may'st thou bud,
And well may'st thou blow,
And well may'st thou bear
Of apples e-now!
Hats full! Caps full!
Good bushel sacks full!
My pockets too, Hurrah!
 Wassail!

Here's to thee, old apple tree,
Here's to thee, old apple tree!
Give us a crop
Of good apples ripe,
And Red and well rounded
The good juicy type!
Hats full! Caps full!

Good bushel sacks full!
My pockets too, Hurrah!
 Wassail!

Here's to thee, old apple tree,
Here's to thee, old apple tree!
Here is our ale,
Now drink of it well,
And give us good apples
Of which we can tell!
Hats full! Caps full!
Good bushel sacks full!
My pockets too, Hurrah!
 Wassail!

*Here's To Thee, Old Apple Tree!*
*Traditional English Song*

He is the happiest man who can

connect the end of his life with its beginning.
*Goethe*

Common duties become religious acts when performed with fervor.
*St. Francis of Sales*

And it was observed that in the greatest hurry of business in the kitchen he still preserved his recollection and heavenly-mindedness. "The time of business," said he, "does not with me differ from the time of prayer; and in the noise and clatter of my kitchen, while several persons are

Cinnamon is the bark of the cinnamon tree, and its value can scarcely be estimated. It is one of the oldest spices known to man and is one of the predominant scents used in the incense burned for ritual purposes. The uses of cinnamon in cooking are without number and it is used equally in savory dishes and desserts. It is important for pickling and it is difficult to imagine rice pudding without it.
*Craig Claiborne, An Herb And Spice Cook Book*

New happiness too must be learned to bear.
*Ebner-Eschenbach*

Ding dong! merrily on high
The bells are gaily ringing;
Ding dong! happily reply
The angels all a singing.
Gloria Hosanna in excelsis.

Ding dong! Carol all the bells.
Awake now, do not tarry!
Sing out, sound the good
   nowells,
Jesu is born of Mary.
Gloria Hosanna in excelsis.
*Ding Dong, A Round Accompanied by Singing*

A multitude of small delights constitutes happiness.
*Charles Baudelaire*

I never spoke with God
Nor visited in Heaven
Yet certain am I of the spot
As if the Checks were given.
*Emily Dickinson*

# Christmas Rice Pudding

(*Arroz dulce*)

| | |
|---|---|
| ½  cup raw rice | ¼  teaspoon salt |
| 2  cups boiling water | 1  egg |
| 1½ cups milk or cocoanut milk | 1  tablespoon butter |
| ¼  cup sugar | 1  teaspoon vanilla extract |
| ½  cup seedless raisins | |

Wash rice. Put in a saucepan with the boiling water and boil 15 minutes, stirring occasionally. Drain and rinse under cold running water. Scald milk in top of double boiler over boiling water. Add the rice, sugar, raisins, and salt, and cook, covered, until rice is tender—about 40 minutes. Beat egg well, and add to it 2 heaping tablespoons of the rice mixture. Mix well and pour back into remaining rice mixture in the double boiler. Cook, stirring constantly for 1 minute. Add butter and stir until melted. Remove from heat. Add vanilla and mix well. Serve warm or cold.

This recipe may be used with cocoanut milk, but it is equally as delicious as plain American rice pudding when cow's milk is used. (Cocoanut milk may be purchased in stores in Spanish sections or may be made by soaking a package of dry cocoanut for 1 hour in 1½ cups water and then straining it.)

Serves 6.

Joy to the world! the Lord is
   come;
Let earth receive her King;
Let every heart prepare Him
   room,
And heaven and nature sing,
And heaven and nature sing,
And heaven, and heaven and
   nature sing.

Joy to the earth! the Saviour
   reigns;
Let men their songs employ;
While fields and floods, rocks,
   hills, and plains
Repeat the sounding joy,
Repeat the sounding joy,
Repeat, repeat the sounding joy.
*Isaac Watts, Joy To The World*

The greatest blessing is created and enjoyed at the same moment.
*Epicurus*

Wassail, wassail, to our town
The cup is white, the ale is
   brown;
The cup is made of the ashen
   tree,
And so is the ale of the good
   barley.
*Mother Goose*

Jesus, our brother, kind and
good,
Was humbly born in a stable
rude.
The friendly beasts around Him
stood,
Jesus, our brother, kind and
good.

"I," said the donkey, all shaggy
and brown,
"I carried His mother up hill
and down,
I carried her safely to Bethle'm
town."
"I," said the donkey, all shaggy
and brown.

"I," said the cow, all white and
red,
"I gave Him my manger for a
bed,
I gave Him my hay to pillow
His head."
"I," said the cow, all white and
red.

"I," said the sheep with the
curly horn,
"I gave Him my wool for a
blanket warm,
He wore my coat on Christmas
morn."
"I," said the sheep with the
curly horn.

# Twelfth Night Cake

| | |
|---|---|
| 1 cup shortening | ½ teaspoon salt |
| 2⅔ cups sugar | 6 beaten egg whites |
| 1½ cups milk | 2 teaspoons vanilla |
| 5½ cups flour | |
| 5 teaspoons baking powder | |

Cream shortening and sugar. Add milk alternately
with sifted dry ingredients. Fold in beaten egg whites.
Add vanilla. Bake in three 9-inch greased layer pans
at 375° for about 30 minutes. Frost the cake with any
desired white icing and top it with a crown of gum-
drops.

"I," said the dove from the
rafters high,
"I cooed Him to sleep, so He
would not cry
We cooed Him to sleep, my mate
and I."
"I," said the dove from the
rafters high.

So every beast, by some good
spell,
In the stable rude was glad to
tell
Of the gift he gave Immanuel,
The gift he gave Immanuel.

*The Friendly Beasts, English Twelfth
Century Song*

Ever since the period of twelve
days from the Nativity to Epi-
phany was declared a festal time
by the Church in 567, this time
has been celebrated as the big
holiday of the year in most
countries where Christianity
exists. In medieval England the
twelve days were marked by an
unbroken succession of gaieties.
There were jousts, banqueting,
caroling, and "mumming," which
originally was a kind of pan-
tomime dance performed by
groups who were both costumed
and masked. Minstrels and jug-
glers made music and mirth.

*Haig and Regina Shekerjian, A Book
Of Christmas Carols*

Up the Ladder
And down the Wall,
A halfpenny Loaf
Will serve us all.
You find milk
And I'll find flour.
And we'll have a pudding
In half an hour.

*Mother Goose*

Fan the flame of hilarity with the
wing of friendship; and pass the
rosy wine.

*Charles Dickens*

It is only in our eyes that animals
grow old.

*G. C. Lichtenberg*

Smell of bread. Homely words.
The light faded
In the snow's whirling ashes.
*Dag Hammarskjöld, Markings*

Wake up, Pierre, awaken,
Come hear the music gay!
How can you sleep this morning,
When dawn brings such a day?
Can't you hear the shepherds
  singing?
Can't you see the star so bright?
Joyful sounds the music ringing,
With the dawn comes rosy light.
Come and join the happy singing,
Come see the pretty sight!
O come, Pierre, I beg you,
Let's go and join them there!
They go to little Jesu;
He lies in stable bare.
Let us run and hurry after
All our friends who go there
  too!
Little Jesu, darling baby,
We will sing a song to you!
Mary, mother of the baby,
How blessed is she too!

*Noel Haut, Haut, Peyrot, An Old
Christmas Carol*

The custom of wassailing the
fruit trees was common throughout England. In Sussex the
wassailing took place on Christmas Eve. In Devonshire it was
New Year's Eve when the farmer
and his men went out to the

# Christmas Day Bread
(*Christstollen*)

Christstollen needs plenty of room so that the shape of
the child in swaddling clothes will surely be seen in the
folds of dough.

| | |
|---|---|
| 1 cake yeast | ½ teaspoon nutmeg |
| 1 tablespoon sugar | 1 cup raisins |
| ¼ cup lukewarm water | 1 cup currants |
| 1 cup shortening | ½ cup blanched |
| 1¼ cups sugar |    almonds |
| 2 eggs | ½ cup chopped citron |
| 2 cups scalded milk | 1½ teaspoons lemon |
| 6 cups flour |    extract |
| 1 teaspoon salt | |

Dissolve yeast and sugar in warm water. Cover and
allow to bubble up. Cream shortening and sugar. Add
eggs and scalded milk cooled to lukewarm. Alternate
with flour sifted with salt and nutmeg. Add yeast mixture. Add fruits and flavoring. Knead until smooth.
Cover and let dough rise to double its bulk. Knead
dough again. Shape dough into ropes about 1½ inches
in diameter. For each large stollen make one rope 3
feet long and two that are 2½ feet long. Braid the
dough, bringing the braid to a point at either end.
Place the braid on a greased cookie sheet. Bake at 400°
for 25 minutes or until brown. This recipe will make
two large stollen.

orchard with a large jug of cider.
There, encircling one of the best-
bearing trees, they drank a toast
and then fired their guns in
conclusion. Dancing and singing
around the trees, or beating upon
them to make them bear, was
common in all of these countries.
Some Tyrolese farmers would go
out on Christmas Eve, knock
with bent fingers upon their
trees, and bid them all wake up
and bear fruit.

*Haig and Regina Shekerjian, A Book
Of Christmas Carols*

When I hear music I fear no
danger, I am invulnerable, I see
no foe. I am related to the earliest
times, and to the latest.
*Henry David Thoreau*

Sound is more than sense.
*Logan Pearsall Smith*

We must make our homes centres
of compassion and forgive
endlessly.
*Mother Teresa of Calcutta*

Every believer in this world of ours must be a spark of light, a center of love, a vivifying leaven amidst his fellowmen.
*Pope John XXIII*

The Angel's Bread is made
The Bread of man today:
The Living Bread from Heaven
With figures doth away:
O wondrous gift indeed!
The poor and lowly may
Upon their Lord and Master feed.
*St. Thomas Aquinas, Matins Hymn for Corpus Christi*

Gentyll bakers, make good breade for good bread doth comfort, confyrme, & doth stablushhe a mannes herte. Mery herte & mynde, the which is in reste & qyetness without adversyte & to moche worldly busyness causeth a man to lyve longe, & to loke yongly, althou he be aged.
*Andrewe Boorde, A Dyetary of Helth*

Everything unnatural is imperfect.
*Napoleon*

There's a star in the East on
  Christmas morn,
Rise up, shepherd, and follow!
It will lead to the place where
  the Saviour's born,
Rise up, shepherd, and follow!
Leave your sheep and leave your
  lambs;
Rise up, shepherd, and follow!

# Christmas Bread

| | |
|---|---|
| 4 cups milk | follow directions on package) |
| 3½ cups sugar | |
| 3½ teaspoons salt | 1⅓ cup warm water for yeast |
| 11 eggs | |
| 1 cup butter, melted | 2½ pounds raisins |
| 7 packages of yeast. (If dry yeast is used | 16–17 cups flour (begin with 14 cups and add remainder as needed.) |

Raisins can be separated and soaked in ¼ to ½ cup milk. This milk is used in addition to the above 4 cups.

Scald milk. Add sugar and salt. When cool, add beaten eggs and melted butter. Dissolve yeast in warm water and add to the milk mixture. Be sure milk is cool enough before adding yeast. Add raisins to the milk mixture and then add all to the flour and beat. Some flour may have to be added, but the batter should be a little sticky. Let rise to double in size and then punch down; make into loaves. Place in greased bread loaf pans. Let rise in pans until double in size. Bake at 325° for about 50 minutes.

Makes 5 loaves, cakelike consistency.

If you take good heed to the
  angel's words,
Rise up, shepherd, and follow!
You'll forget your flocks, you'll
  forget your herds,
Rise up, shepherd, and follow!
Leave your sheep and leave
  your lambs;
Rise up, shepherd, and follow!
*Rise Up, Shepherd, And Follow, An American Negro Spiritual*

Children and subjects are much seldomer in the wrong than parents and kings.
*Lord Chesterfield*

To me, fair friend, you never
  can be old,
For as you were when first your
  eye I ey'd,
Such seems your beauty still.
*Shakespeare*

It is this sense of family which gives great strength to a monastic group. Any man anywhere, any group of men anywhere, could become monks. But you may be sure they would endeavor very soon to get in touch with a tradition, either through living monks or through texts, in order to pick up the thread of continuity.
*Matthew Kelty, Aspects of The Monastic Calling*

For this good food
and joy renewed
We praise your name, O Lord.
*A French Thanksgiving*

Monastic life is no picnic.
*Matthew Kelty, Aspects of the Monastic Calling*

*Prudentia*, significantly called the "mother" of all other virtues—
. . . cannot be perfected except by an attitude of "silent contemplation" of reality, during which the egocentric interests of man are at least temporarily silenced. Only on the basis of this magnanimous kind of prudence can we achieve justice, fortitude, and *temperantia*, which means knowing when enough is enough.
*E. F. Schumacher, Small Is Beautiful*

We have all these impossible desires within us as a mark of our destination, and they are good for us when we no longer hope to accomplish them.
*Simone Weil, Waiting For God*

Historical evidence would indicate that very few key inventions have been made by men who had to spend all their energy overcoming the immediate pressures of survival. The first genetic experiments, which led a hundred years later to high-yield agricultural crops, took place in the

# Monk's Marvelous Molasses Drink

| | |
|---|---|
| 8 tablespoons powdered milk | 2 cups water |
| 6 tablespoons unsulfured molasses | |

Mix well the powdered milk with 1 cup water in a small pot. Bring to a boil, continuing to stir. When boiled, add molasses and 1 cup cold water. Stir and mix well. Serve warm in the winter, especially at night. Chill and serve cold in the summer.

Makes 2 glasses or cups.

peace of a European monastery.
*Donella H. Meadows, Limits to Growth*

The spirit cannot endure the body when overfed but, if underfed, the body cannot endure the spirit.
*St. Francis of Sales*

The simplicity of the monastic way of life is bound to stand out in such a complicated world as ours. We are a society geared to sensory overkill. Monks have something to share when it comes to the rediscovery of simple enjoyment—the smell of hot coffee,

or freshly mown hay, the sight of soft, early morning sunlight falling on the chapel floor. Monastic life is a sapiential life, a life of growing in wisdom. Its wisdom is nothing highblown or esoteric —it is rooted in the human. "Sapere" means to taste, so a cookbook is a very appropriate way to share the wisdom of monastic simplicity.
*Sister Donald Corcoran, OSB*

Aging people should know that their lives are not mounting and unfolding but that an inexorable inner process forces the contraction of life. For a young person

it is almost a sin—and certainly a danger—to be too much occupied with himself; but for the aging person it is a duty and a necessity to give serious attention to himself.
*Carl Jung*

There's more time than life.
*Mexican Saying quoted by Cesar Chavez*

"Take some more tea," the March Hare said to Alice, very earnestly. "I've had nothing yet," Alice replied in an offended tone: "so I can't take more." "You mean you can't take less," said the Hatter: "it's very easy to take more than nothing."
*Lewis Carroll, Alice's Adventures in Wonderland*

To fill the hour, and leave no crevice for a repentance or an approval—that is happiness.
*Ralph Waldo Emerson*

# Spring

A swarm of bees in May
Is worth a load of hay;
A swarm of bees in June
Is worth a silver spoon;
A swarm of bees in July
Is not worth a fly.
*Old English Saying*

Many soups that evolved through the centuries in the French provinces are based more on vegetables than on meats or even meat stocks, and are frankly described as "healthy": *potages de santé*. Their recipes are ancient, as basic as the need for cabin-bound men to go out with their livestock in the first days of spring and gather the grasses and roots of the awakening meadows. These soups depend on spinach and sorrel, and all the herbs, and mushrooms, and fresh milk and cream and butter, all tasting perennially and incredibly delicious after the long dark months of eating stored roots like turnips and potatoes, and cabbages and onions and garlic.
*M. F. K. Fisher, The Cooking of Provincial France*

God gives food to every bird, but does not throw it into the nest.
*Montenegrin Proverb*

Nothing on earth is so thrilling, so terrifying, as the power of our hands to keep us or mar us. All that man does is the hand alive, the hand manifest, creating and destroying, itself the interest of order and demolition. It moves a stone, and the universe undergoes

# Minestrone

Minestrone is simply the Italian term for a green vegetable soup. Since this recipe calls for fresh vegetables, it is inestimably better than the best canned minestrone available.

Cut up fine any vegetables available (with the exception of tomatoes or beets). The most frequently employed in Italy are green cabbage leaves, green peas, zucchini, and potatoes, but almost anything can be added, including parsley, spinach, and so on. In the winter, dried beans or peas can be used. Add chopped onion, a clove of garlic whole (or minced if you prefer) and a pinch each of oregano, thyme and basil. Salt and pepper to taste. Cook about 1 hour in ⅓ more water than needed to cover the quantity of vegetables used. Cook longer if dried vegetables are used. Two or three minutes before serving, add a handful of very fine noodles if desired. Just before serving, add 1 or 2 tablespoons of olive oil, and mix well into the soup.

a readjustment. It breaks a clod, and a new beauty bursts forth in fruits and flowers, and the sea of fertility flows over the desert.
*Helen Keller*

June 8, 1838. [Age 35] A man must have aunts and cousins, must buy carrots and turnips, must have barn and woodshed, must go to market and to the blacksmith's shop, must saunter and sleep and be inferior and silly.
*Ralph Waldo Emerson*

If wise men never erred, fools would have to despair.
*Goethe*

Beautiful Soup, so rich and green,
Waiting in a hot tureen!
Who for such dainties would not stoop?
Soup of the evening, beautiful Soup!
*Lewis Carroll, Alice in Wonderland*

Seldom are hunger and thirst together.
*Irish Proverb*

Oh thrice and four times happy those who plant cabbages!
*François Rabelais*

I have never been able to school
  my eyes
Against young April's blue
  surprise.
*Charles Leo O'Donnell, Wonder*

Pease-porridge hot, pease-
porridge cold,
Pease-porridge in the pot,
nine days old.
*Mother Goose*

Thank you for the food we eat,
Thank you for the world so
  sweet;
Thank you for the birds that sing,
Thank you God for everything.
Amen.
*Children's Table Grace*

Life, it seems to me, is worth living, but only if we avoid the
amusements of grown-up people.
*Robert Lynd*

Because the monk speaks little,
he is a good listener and watcher.
How much the birds teach him!
About frugality and simplicity
and grace. About finding food
where one might not look for it.

# Oatmeal and Broth

1 tablespoon (approxi-
  mately) oatmeal per
  person
pinch salt

sugar to taste
broth or vegetable
  bouillon

Mix the dry ingredients together and dilute in broth or
bouillon. Let stand for 2 hours unless the quick-cooking
variety of oatmeal is used. Cook 1 to 5 minutes depending on the variety of oatmeal used. Add enough broth
to make a more liquid mixture. The quantity of broth
added depends on taste. Some prefer the dish almost
soupy; others like it firm. But there must be sufficient
liquid to allow for the swelling of the oatmeal.

About the grubbiness of life—
hunting for insects, building nests,
sometimes squawking unbearably.
They teach us that the breathless
grace of flight and song is sometimes found together with down-
right meanness.
*Brother Patrick Francis*

Spring has many American faces.
There are cities where it will
come and go in a day and coun-
ties where it hangs around and
never quite gets there. . . . Summer is drawn blinds in Louisiana,
long winds in Wyoming, shade of
elms and maples in New England.
. . . Autumn is the American

season. In Europe the leaves turn
yellow or brown, and fall. Here
they take fire on the trees and
hang there flaming. We think this
frost-fire is a portent somehow:
a promise that the continent has
given us. Life, too, we think, is
capable of taking fire in this
country; of creating beauty never
seen.
*Archibald MacLeish, Sweet Land of
Liberty*

Much has been said by all manner of people in praise of enthusiasm. The important point is that
enthusiasm is ephemeral, and
hence unserviceable for the long

haul. One can hardly conceive of
a more unhealthy and wasteful
state of affairs than where faith
and dedication are requisite for
the performance of unmiraculous
everyday activities.
*Eric Hoffer*

To take away the taste of Burning from a Pottage. Take a fresh
pot and put your pottage therein,
then take a little yeast and tie it
in a white cloth and put it into
your pot and do not let it remain
there long.
*The Goodman of Paris (Le Ménagier
de Paris)*

Spring is the usual period for
house-cleaning and removing the
dust and dirt which, notwith-
standing all precautions, will ac-
cumulate during the winter
months from dust, smoke, gas,
etc.
*Mrs. Beeton's Household Management*

Man's happiness does not lie in
freedom, but in the acceptance of
a duty.
*André Gide*

A line, a shade, a color—their fiery expressiveness. The language of flowers, mountains, shores, human bodies: the interplay of light and shade in a look, the aching beauty of a neckline, the grail of the white crocus on the alpine meadow in the morning

## Mixed Salad

(*Salade mélangée*)

| | |
|---|---|
| 1½ cups fresh green peas | parsley, salt, pepper |
| 1½ cups green beans, cut in 1-inch slices | 1 large green pepper, sliced |
| 1 small onion, minced oil and vinegar dressing | 3 or 4 tomatoes |
| | 3 hard-boiled eggs |

Cook peas and green beans. Drain and rinse briefly in cold water. Toss still-warm peas and beans with onion, dressing, seasonings, and green pepper. Chill.

Serve either on a platter surrounded with rings of sliced tomatoes and sliced eggs *or* stuff salad into hollowed-out tomatoes, surrounded by egg slices. Good with mayonnaise.

Serves 6.

sunshine—words in a transcendental language of the senses.
*Dag Hammarskjöld, Markings*

One is never tired of painting, because you have to set down not what you know already, but what you have just discovered.
*William Hazlitt*

*Blessing of Herbs.* You have made heaven and earth, and all things visible and invisible, and have enriched the earth with plants and trees for the use of men and animals. You appointed each species to bring forth fruit of its own kind, not only to serve as food for living creatures, but also as medicine for sick bodies.

With mind and body, we earnestly implore You in your goodness, to bless these various herbs and add to their natural powers the healing power of your grace. May they keep off disease and adversity from the men and beasts who use them in our name.
*An Old Russian Prayer*

According to the Spanish proverb, four persons are wanted to make a good salad: a spendthrift for oil, a miser for vinegar, a counsellor for salt, and a madman to stir all up.
*Abraham Hayward, The Art of Dining*

Art is man added to nature.
*Francis Bacon*

The butterfly, a cabbage-white,
(His honest idiocy of flight)
Will never now, it is too late,
Master the art of flying straight,
Yet has—who knows so well as
I?—
A just sense of how not to fly:
He lurches here and there by
guess
And God and hope and hopelessness.
Even the aerobatic swift
Has not his flying-crooked gift.
*Robert Graves*

There is a logic of colors, and it is with this alone, and not with the logic of the brain, that the painter should conform.
*Paul Cézanne*

To live is like to love—all reason is against it, and all healthy instinct for it.
*Samuel Butler*

Wherever water flows it will find a way.
*Russian Proverb*

The universal points
Are shrunk into a flower;
Between its delicate joints
Chaos keeps no power.
*Elinor Wylie*

I suspect that the child plucks its
first flower with an insight into its
beauty and significance which the
subsequent botanist never retains.
*Henry David Thoreau*

The Little Prince crossed the
   desert and met with only one
   flower with 3 petals, a flower
   of no account at all.
"Good morning," said the Little
   Prince.
"Good morning," said the flower.
"Where are the men?" the Little
   Prince asked, politely.
The flower had once seen a
   caravan passing.
"Men?" she echoed. "I think
   there are six or seven of them
   in existence. I saw them,
   several years ago. But one
   never knows where to find
   them. The wind blows them
   away. They have no roots."
"Goodbye," said the Little
   Prince.
"Goodbye," said the flower.
*Antoine De Saint-Exupery, The Little
Prince*

# Raw Spinach-Mushroom Salad

| | |
|---|---|
| spinach, torn | diced carrots (optional) |
| mushrooms (fresh), | oil and vinegar dressing |
| whole or sliced depending | with a dash of tamari |
| on size | or soy sauce |

Nonvegetarians can sprinkle crisp bacon bits over this.

Plants bear witness to the reality
of roots.
*Maimonides*

Life was meant to be lived, and
   curiosity must be kept alive.
One must never, for whatever
   reason, turn his back on life.
*Eleanor Roosevelt*

Art is the only clean thing on
earth, except holiness.
*Joris Karl Huysmans, Les Foules de
Lourdes*

He who shall hurt the little wren
Shall never be belov'd by men.
He who the ox to wrath has
   mov'd
Shall never be by women lov'd
The wanton Boy that kills the fly

Shall feel the spider's enmity.
He who torments the chafer's
   sprite
Weaves a bower in endless night.
The caterpillar on the leaf
Repeats to thee thy mother's
   grief.
Kill not the moth nor butterfly,
For the Last Judgment draweth
   nigh.
He who shall train the horse to
   war
Shall never pass the polar bar.
The beggar's dog and widow's
   cat,
Feed them, and thou wilt grow
   fat.
*William Blake, Auguries of Innocence*

It is a great obstacle to happiness
to expect too much.
*Bernard de Fontenelle, 1657–1757*

Rise early. Eat simple food. Take
plenty of exercise. Never fear a
little fatigue. Let not children
be dressed in tight clothes; it is
necessary their limbs and muscles
should have full play, if you wish
for either health or beauty.

Avoid the necessity of a physician, if you can, by careful
attention to your diet. Eat what
best agrees with your system, and
resolutely abstain from what
hurts you, however well you may
like it. A few days' abstinence,
and cold water for a beverage,
has driven off many an approach-
ing disease.
*Mrs. Child, The American Frugal
Housewife*

The hen is an egg's way of producing another egg.
*Samuel Butler*

Blue! Gentle cousin of the
   forest-green,
Married to green in all the
   sweetest flowers—
Forget-me-not—the blue bell—
   and that Queen
Of secrecy, the violet.
*John Keats*

Silently one by one, in the infinite
   meadows of heaven
Blossomed the lovely stars, the
   forget-me-nots of the angels.
*Henry Wadsworth Longfellow,
Evangeline*

If some one loves a flower, of
which just one single blossom
grows in all the millions of stars,
it is enough to make him happy
just to look at the stars. He can
say to himself: "Somewhere, my
flower is there." But if the sheep
eats the flower in one moment all
his stars will be darkened. . . .
And you think that is not
important!
*Antoine De Saint-Exupery, The Little
Prince*

We may live without poetry,
 · music, and art;
We may live without conscience,
  and live without heart;

# Tomatoes Stuffed with Eggs
(*Farce aux oeufs*)

| | | |
|---|---|---|
| 6 | slices bread, diced | chopped parsley |
| ½ | cup milk | chopped chives |
| 2 | hard-boiled eggs, diced | dill (optional) |
| | salt, pepper | 6 tomatoes |

Moisten bread with milk; use more milk if necessary to get bread thoroughly soft. Combine all ingredients except tomatoes and cook over low heat until excess liquid has evaporated. Stuff hollowed-out tomatoes.
   Serves 6.

We may live without friends; we
  may live without books;
But civilized man cannot live
  without cooks.
*Edward Robert Bulwer, 1st Earl of
Lytton*

For apart from Him who can
eat or who can have enjoyment.
*Ecclesiastes 2:25,* RSV

Besides the near-primitive boiling, braising and refreshing of vegetables, there are countless other ways of making them into dishes that are hardly less ancient. A *ratatouille* from Provence, for instance, has been served for

many years in most of the countires of the Near East and the Mediterranean basin and is made from the same basic ingredients: eggplant, tomatoes, onions, olive oil. It will vary a little not only with the cook but with the herbs and materials available, but it is rare to find an end result that is not highly edible. A *ratatouille* improves with age, unlike most vegetable concoctions, and can be reheated or served cold for several days.
*M. F. K. Fisher, The Cooking of
Provincial France*

The very best and utmost of attainment in life is to remain still and let God act and speak in thee.
*Meister Eckhart*

I once ate a pea.
*George (Beau) Brummell, when
asked at dinner if he never ate
vegetables.*

We grow weary when idle.
*James Boswell*

Blest be those feasts with simple
  plenty crown'd,
Where all the ruddy family
  around
Laugh at the jests or pranks that
  never fail,
Or sigh with pity at some mourn-
  ful tale,
Or press the bashful stranger to
  his food,
And learn the luxury of doing
  good.
*Oliver Goldsmith, The Traveller*

A little dish oft furnishes enough,
And sure enough is equal to a
  feast.
*Henry Fielding*

Home is not where you live but
where they understand you.
*Christian Morgenstern*

As the dressing, so the appetite.
*Latvian Proverb*

If ever two were one, then
  surely we.
If ever man were lov'd by wife,

# Baked Tomatoes with Eggs

(*Oeufs aux tomates*)

For each serving:

| | |
|---|---|
| butter | salt, pepper |
| 1 tomato | 2 eggs |
| parsley, grated onion, garlic powder | ¼ cup grated Swiss cheese |

(This dish can be prepared in individual ovenproof dishes or in one large dish.)

Butter or oil baking dish. Place thick tomato slices in dish, and season them. Bake at 350° until heated through and tender. When the tomatoes are cooked, rearrange them gently to make "holes" in which to put eggs. Break eggs directly into baking dish. Sprinkle with grated cheese and place under broiler 4 inches from flame until eggs are cooked and cheese is melted and browned.

then thee;
If ever wife was happy in a man,
Compare with me ye women if
  you can.
*Anne Bradstreet, c. 1612–1672
To My Dear and Loving Husband*

The "mother cuisine" of Italy assimilated many products of the New World and helped introduce them to the Old. It is hard to imagine modern Italian cooking without the tomato, yet no European had ever set eyes on it before Cortez conquered Mexico. The first Italian description of a tomato, in 1554, called it *pomo d'oro* or "golden apple"

(spelled *pomodoro* today). And in fact the first tomato seen in Europe was yellow in color, and about the size of a cherry. It took nearly two centuries for the Italians to develop new, bigger, red varieties and to use the tomato regularly in cooking; it was used at first as a salad vegetable.
*Waverley Root, The Cooking of Italy*

Good food should be grown on whole soil, be eaten whole, unprocessed, and garden fresh.
*Helen and Scott Nearing,
Living the Good Life*

Throw open wide your senses,

longing intensely with each of them for all which is God.
*Hadewijch of Antwerp, 12th century Beguine*

The Eagle soars in the summit
  of Heaven,
The Hunter with his dogs pursues
  his circuit.
O perpetual revolution of con-
  figured stars,
O perpetual recurrence of determined seasons,
O world of spring and autumn,
  birth and dying!
*T. S. Eliot, Two Choruses From 'The Rock'*

There are persons who have so far outgrown their catechism as to believe that their only duty is to themselves.
*Samuel Johnson*

I do not hunger for a well-stored mind, I only wish to live my life, and find My heart in unison with all mankind.
*Lord Randolph Spencer Churchill*

Let the brethren serve one another.
*Rule of St. Benedict*

No man can be wise on an empty stomach.
*George Eliot*

A smiling face is half the meal.
*Latvian Proverb*

Babies and small children are pure beauty, love, joy—the truest in this world. But the thorns are there of night watches, of illnesses, of infant perversities and contrariness. There are glimpses of heaven and hell.
*Dorothy Day, On Pilgrimage*

In homes where silence is lived, the child finds it easy and comfortable to turn to it. In a large and noisy family (like my own) the period of hush that begins every meal sweeps like a healing wind over all the cross-currents that have built up in the previous hours and leaves the household clean and sweet.
*Elise Boulding, Children and Solitude*

Guard the ground well, for it belongs to God;

# Apples and Rice-with-Onions
(*Riz aux oignons*)

| | |
|---|---|
| 4 to 6 apples, peeled or unpeeled, sliced | 2 onions, sliced |
| ¼ cup sugar or honey | ½ cup rice |
| | ½ cup water |

Cook the apples, using as little water as possible, sweetening at the end of cooking.

In another pan, brown the sliced onions in oil or margarine, cooking and stirring gently until just golden. Add rice and water in equal quantities (½ cup for 4 servings) and cook slowly. After the water has boiled, reduce heat and let simmer until done (about 20 minutes for white rice). Watch it the last few minutes; all the liquid should be gone, but it will burn quickly after this point. If the rice is not done when the liquid is gone, add a little more water as necessary. More water and more time will be needed for brown rice. Before serving, mix well so that the onions are distributed throughout. Pile the rice-with-onions on a platter bordered with the cooked apples and serve with some good cheese and a salad.

Serves 4.

Root out the hateful and the bitter weed,
And from the harvest of thy
Heart's good seed
The hungry shall be fed, the
naked clad,
And love's infection, leaven-like,
shall spread
Till all creation feeds from heavenly bread.
*Kenneth Boulding*

Plain fare gives as much pleasure as a costly diet, while bread and water confer the highest possible pleasure when they are brought to hungry lips.
*Epicurus*

She had been so wicked that in all her life she had only done one good deed—given an onion to a beggar. So she went to hell. As she lay in torment she saw the onion, lowered down from heaven by an angel. She caught hold of it. He began to pull her up. The other damned saw what was happening and caught hold of it too. She was indignant and cried, "Let go—it's my onion," and as soon as she said "My onion" the stalk broke and she fell back into the flames.
*E. M. Forster, The Hill of Devi*

Grief can take care of itself, but to get the full value of a joy you must have somebody to divide it with.
*Mark Twain*

April prepares her green traffic light and the world thinks Go.
*Christopher Morley, John Mistletoe*

Well loved he garlic, onions, and eke leeks,
And for to drinken strong wine, red as blood.
*Geoffrey Chaucer, Canterbury Tales*

The world is wide; not two days are alike, nor even two hours; neither was there ever two leaves of a tree alike since the creation of the world; and the genuine productions of art, like those of nature, are all distinct from each other.
*John Constable*

Exuberance is beauty.
*William Blake*

The real value of love is the increased general vitality it produces.
*Paul Valéry*

The monk finally seeks solitude and silence . . . because he knows

# Vegetable-Noodle Casserole

1 12-oz. package broad egg noodles
2 cups diced eggplant
2 medium tomatoes, sliced
1 green pepper, chopped
1 onion, chopped

1 tablespoon chopped parsley
garlic powder, salt, pepper
1 cup yellow cheese, coarsely grated

Prepare noodles according to package directions and drain. Sauté vegetables and seasonings gently in oil until softened. Combine noodles, vegetable mixture, and 1 cup cheese in a buttered casserole dish. Sprinkle top with Parmesan. Bake at 350° until heated through, about 30 to 45 minutes.
    Serves 6.

that the real fruit of his vocation is union with God in love and contemplation. An apt saying of the Moslem Sufis comes to mind here: The hen does not lay eggs in the market place.
*Thomas Merton*

If an Arab in the desert were suddenly to discover a spring in his tent, and so would always be able to have water in abundance, how fortunate he would consider himself—so too, when a man, who as a physical being is always turned toward the outside, thinking that his happiness lies outside him,

finally turns inward and discovers that the source is within him; not to mention his discovery that the source is his relation to God.
*Sören Kierkegaard*

The French housewife's way of holding the newness and greenness of the fresh vegetables is simplicity itself: boil (or blanch, in cooking terminology) green things like beans in a large quantity of boiling water. Then plunge them when barely done into an equally large amount of very cold water. This second process is called "refreshing"

and the end result reflects the name. Drained, the beans will have kept all their flavor and color, and will be ready for last-minute preparation such as reheating in butter in a skillet, before they are served.
*M. F. K. Fisher, The Cooking of Provincial France*

It is God's gift to man that every one should eat and drink and take pleasure in all his toil.
*Ecclesiastes 3:13,* RSV

There are men who are happy without knowing it.
*Vauvenargues*

But from the mountain's grassy
    side
A guiltless feast I bring;
A scrip with herbs and fruits sup-
    plied,
And water from the spring.
*Oliver Goldsmith, The Vicar of
Wakefield*

# Festive Lasagna

*Spaghetti Sauce:*
1 large onion, chopped
1 carrot, thinly sliced
1 clove garlic, cut up
    (optional)
1 12 oz. can tomato pureé

7 cups of canned
    tomatoes
bay leaf
2 pinches oregano
salt, pepper

Gently fry onion, carrot, and garlic in oil. Stir in tomato pureé and strained whole tomatoes. Add bay leaf and oregano. Simmer about 2 hours, stirring to prevent burning as often as necessary until sauce is the desired thickness. Salt sparingly at the last minute. Add pepper if a spicier sauce is desired.

*Lasagna:*
1 lb. lasagna noodles
oil
spaghetti sauce
¾ lb. ricotta or cottage

cheese (ricotta is more
    expensive)
1 lb. mozzarella cheese
wheat germ

Cook noodles according to package directions. Oil bottom of a large baking dish and put in liberal layers in this order: sauce, noodles, sauce, noodles, ricotta or cottage cheese, noodles, sauce. Top with sliced mozzarella cheese, and sprinkle top with wheat germ. Use tomato sauce liberally. Bake at 375° for about 30 minutes.
  Serves 6 to 8.

O Thou who clothest the lilies of
    the field
and feedest the birds of the air,
Who leadest the sheep to pasture
and the hart to the water's side,
Who has multiplied loaves and
    fishes
and converted water to wine.
Do Thou come to our table
as Giver and Guest to dine.
*Blessing of Food with Wine*

Now when someone asked him how it was possible to eat acceptably to the gods, he said, If it is done graciously and fairly and restrainedly and decently, is it not also done acceptably to the gods?
*Epictetus*

I had been hungry, all the Years—
My Noon had Come—to dine—
I trembling drew the Table
    near—
And touched the Curious Wine.
*Emily Dickinson*

Do as adversaries do in law, strive mightily, but eat and drink as friends.
*William Shakespeare, Taming of the Shrew*

Friendship is Love without his wings.
*Lord Byron, L'Amitié Est l'Amore sans Ailes*

One pancake for lunch and half a boiled egg for dinner makes a man at sixty able to do anything a college athlete can do.
*Sir William Osler*

The happiest people seem to be those who have no particular cause for being happy except that they are so.
*W. R. Inge*

He sendeth sun, he sendeth
   shower,
Alike they're needful to the
   flower;
And joys and tears alike are sent
To give the soul fit nourishment.
As comes to me or cloud or sun,
Father! thy will, not mine, be
   done.
*Sarah Flower Adams*

There is nothing which has yet been contrived by man, by which so much happiness is produced as by a good tavern or inn; a tavern chair is the throne of human felicity.
*Samuel Johnson*

I believe it is best to eat just as one is hungry; but a man who is in business, or a man who has a family, must have stated meals.
*Samuel Johnson*

When people come together who have not previously met they are a bit reserved; but when food is introduced there is an immediate change in the atmosphere. The power of the festive table begins

# French Pancakes with Filling
(*Crêpes*)

3 eggs (I always add an extra egg "for the bowl")
1½ cups sifted flour
½ teaspoon salt
1½ cups milk (or 1 cup milk, ½ cup water)
3 tablespoons oil or melted butter

Beat eggs. Beat flour and salt in gradually, then milk, and oil. Dough must "rest," covered and in refrigerator, at least 2 hours; overnight is good. Use a small frying pan, preferably one with low sides, no more than 7 inches in diameter. Oil or butter it for each crêpe. Pour about 3 tablespoons of batter into warm pan and rotate pan to spread batter evenly over surface. Batter should be very thin. (Trial and error will lead to best heat to use, whether to add a few tablespoons of milk to thin batter slightly, etc.) When one side is brown, run spatula around edge of crêpe, then under it, and turn it to brown other side. An athlete can keep 2 pans going; most of us can cook only one crêpe at a time. The best way to keep them moist after they are cooked is to fold them in quarters and stack them. They ought to be quite pliable and unfold easily later.

To fill them with fish or vegetable stuffing, put a few spoonfuls of filling on one side of flat crêpe and roll it up. Rolled crêpes should be heated up quickly in oven at 375° or until all are hot through; serve immediately.

Makes about 12 small crêpes.

to operate, bringing a feeling of gentleness and warmth. What I am trying to convey is that we have to begin somewhere to relate to the environment. How better than with food?
*Alan Hooker, Vegetarian Gourmet Cookery*

One must be fond of people and trust them if one is not to make a mess of life.
*E. M. Forster*

No man can safely speak, unless he who would gladly remain silent.
*Thomas a Kempis*

A monk is a member of a community. Though the calling is basically solitary (monos means alone), it is normally acted out in community, in a monastery. When one thinks of monks one thinks of monasteries.
*Matthew Kelty, Aspects of The Monastic Calling*

To be a Christian is the great thing, not merely to seem one.
*St. Jerome*

And like the fish, swimming in the vast sea and resting in its deeps, and like the bird, boldly mounting high in the sky, so the soul feels its spirit freely moving through the vastness and the depth and the unutterable richnesses of love.

*Beatrice of Nazareth, 12th century Beguine*

Singing is not worth a thing
if the heart sings not the song,
and the heart can never sing
if it brings not love along.

*Harvey Birenbaum*

"When I get my voice back, I'll sing as well as you," the hoarse cuckoo told the nightingale.

*Russian Proverb*

If an animal does something they call it instinct. If we do exactly the same thing for the same reason they call it intelligence. I guess what they mean is that we all make mistakes, but intelligence enables us to do it on purpose.

*Will Cuppy*

Heaven is under our feet as well as over our heads.

*Henry David Thoreau, Walden*

# Rolled Fish Fillets
(*Filets en paupiettes*)

| | |
|---|---|
| 4 fish fillets | 3 tablespoons butter |
| ¾ cup dry white wine or dry vermouth | 3 tablespoons flour |
| "bouquet garni": parsley, thyme, bay leaf | ½ cup cream |
| | salt, pepper |

Roll the fillets and hold with toothpicks. Place them in a saucepan with the wine; add enough water just to cover the fish. Put in the bouquet garni. Heat *without boiling* for about 10 minutes. Place fish fillets on an ovenproof serving platter, and keep warm without cooking further (175° oven). Remove bay leaf and parsley sprig (and thyme, if fresh sprig was used) from cooking liquid. Boil it down if necessary until 1 cup remains. Melt butter and stir the flour in it for a few minutes; then stir in liquid to make a sauce. Turn off heat and stir in the cream; salt and pepper. Spoon sauce onto fish and serve immediately.

Serves 4.

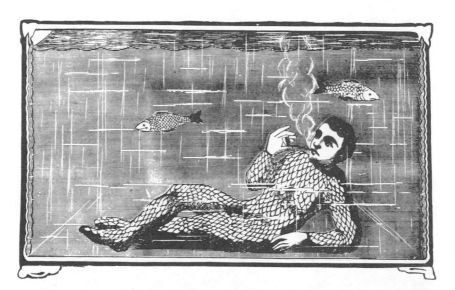

Silence is the universal refuge, the sequel to all dull discourses and all foolish acts, a balm to our every chagrin, as welcome after satiety as after disappointment.
*Henry David Thoreau*

The monk seeks quiet and peace and seclusion not to get away from "the world", but to get closer to it. Not to flee the time's ills, but to heal them.
*Matthew Kelty, Aspects of The Monastic Calling*

Regard all utensils of the monastery as if they were the sacred vessels of the altar.
*Rule of St. Benedict*

It is the chiefest point of happiness that a man is willing to be what he is.
*Erasmus*

The thousand mysteries around us would not trouble but interest us, if only we had cheerful, healthy hearts.
*Friedrich Nietzsche*

A man or a woman enters a monastery for he or she has heard a call stronger than any other. A call that says: "Come, I am Life."
*Brother Victor Antonio*

For a small reward a man will hurry away on a long journey, while for eternal life many will hardly take a single step.
*Thomas a Kempis*

All men cannot be monks; we have different paths allotted to us to mount to the high seat of eternal felicity.
*Cervantes*

The most uncompromising farmer is God Himself.
*Carlo Carretto, Letters from the Desert*

You must drink up the lees also.
*Irish Proverb*

If all the foods were drowned in Noah's flood, the seed was saved.
*L. Stein, Journey into the Self*

"Under-salting" is on the table; "over-salting" is on the cook's back.
*Russian Proverb*

When a thing bores you, do not do it. Do not pursue a fruitless perfection.
*Eugène Delacroix*

# French-Style Fish Fillets

(*Filets aux herbes*)

| | |
|---|---|
| 1 lb. fish fillets | 1 medium onion, chopped |
| ½ cup dry white wine or dry vermouth | parsley, chives, chervil, thyme |
| ½ cup water | 2 tablespoons butter |
| salt, pepper | |

Preheat oven to 350°. Choose a baking dish which can be brought directly to the table. In it place the raw fish fillets. Mix together and then pour in the wine, water, seasonings, onions, and herbs. Dot with butter. Bake 20 to 25 minutes, basting from time to time. Serve from the baking dish, spooning a bit of the juices over each portion.
Serves 4.

He that holds a Frying Pan by the tail may turn it which way he lists.
*English Proverb*

Man is in nature, subject to its dictates and accidents, yet he transcends nature because he lacks the unawareness which makes the animal a part of nature —as one with it.
*Theodosius Dobzhansky*

Mere facility, of course, is no more a guarantee of good taste in cooking than it is in music; but without it, nothing good is possible at all. Technique must be acquired, and, with technique, a love of the very processes of cooking. No artist can work simply for results; he must also like the work of getting them. Not that there isn't a lot of drudgery in any art—and more in cooking than in most—but that if a man has never been pleasantly surprised at the way custard sets or flour thickens, there is not much hope of making a cook of him.
*Father Capon, The Supper Of The Lamb*

Man is meant for happiness and this happiness is in him, in the satisfaction of the daily needs of his existence.
*Leo Tolstoy*

This Bouillabaisse a noble dish is—
A sort of soup, or broth, or brew,
Or hotchpotch of all sorts of fishes,
That Greenwich never could outdo;
Green herbs, red peppers, mussels, saffron,
Soles, onions, garlic, roach, and dace;
All these you eat at Terre's tavern
In that one dish of Bouillabaisse.
*William Makepeace Thackeray, Ballad of Bouillabaisse*

If a thing is worth doing, it is worth doing badly.
*G. K. Chesterton*

The kind of work we do does not make us holy but we may make it holy.
*Meister Eckhart*

In the morning be first vp, and in the euening last to go to bed, for they that sleepe catch no fish.
*English Proverb, 16th Century*

Faith gives by itself what it promises.
*Ernst von Feuchtersleben*

# Tuna-Potato Casserole

6 to 8 potatoes
  (more if very small
  young potatoes)
2 6½-oz. cans tuna
  chunks

wheat germ if desired
white sauce
  (4 tablespoons of flour,
  2 tablespoons of butter,
  2 cups of yogurt)

Steam potatoes in jackets (young potatoes, preferably) and peel and slice while still firm. Make layers in large casserole of potatoes, chunks of tuna, wheat germ; repeat layers as often as needed. Pour in plenty of white sauce made with yogurt. Top with plenty of wheat germ. Bake in 375° oven about 45 minutes. Keep dish covered for most of the baking time so wheat germ does not burn.
    Serves 6.

After silence that which comes nearest to expressing the inexpressible is music.
*Aldous Huxley*

Sunrise is an event that calls forth solemn music in the very depth of man's nature, as if one's whole being had to attune itself to the cosmos and praise God for the new day, praise Him in the name of all the creatures that ever were or ever will be. I look at the rising sun and feel that now upon me falls the responsibility of seeing what all my ancestors have seen, in the Stone Age and even before it, praising God before me.

Whether or not they praised Him then, for themselves, they must praise Him now in me. When the sun rises each one of us is summoned by the living and the dead to praise God.
*Thomas Merton*

Perpetual inspiration is as necessary to the life of goodness, holiness and happiness as perpetual respiration is necessary to animal life.
*William Law*

An ancient monk once said "The monk is one who is separated

from all and yet united to all." The monastic vocation is built on this apparent contradiction.
*An Ancient Monk*

O Thou, who kindly dost provide
For every creature's want!
We bless thee, God of Nature wide,
For all thy goodness lent:
And, if it please thee, Heavenly Guide,
May never worse be sent;
But whether granted, or denied,
Lord, bless us with content!
Amen!
*Robert Burns, A Grace Before Dinner*

To speak in literature with the perfect rectitude and insouciance of the movement of animals, and the unimpeachableness of sentiment of trees in the woods and grass by the roadside, is the flawless triumph of art.
*Walt Whitman*

He who has the courage to laugh is almost as much the master of the world as he who is ready to die.
*Giacomo Leopardi*

In fulness there is no forget-fulness.
*English Proverb*

Frugality is one of the most beautiful and joyful words in the English language, and yet it is one that we are culturally cut off from understanding and enjoying. The consumption society has made us feel that happiness lies in having things, and has failed to teach us the happiness of not having things.
*Elise Boulding, "Women, Frugality and the Planetary Household"*

He that sets the bread in the ouen naughtily, draws out his Batch crusht and ill-fauoured: and as one rews, so let him drinke; as men plot, so let them proue.
*W. S. Countryman's Commonweal*

In Holy Communion we have Christ under the appearance of

# Save-the-Stale-Bread  Casserole
(*Pain perdu au gruyère*)

| | |
|---|---|
| 2  cups milk | up to ½ loaf stale bread |
| 3  beaten eggs | 1  cup grated Gruyère or |
| butter for bread | Swiss cheese |

Preheat oven to 350°. Scald milk and stir slowly into beaten eggs. Butter the slices of bread, then dip them into milk mixture. Place slices on buttered baking dish; cover generously with cheese. Bake about 25 minutes.
Serve 2 slices per person.

bread. In our work we find him under the appearance of flesh and blood. It is the same Christ.
*Mother Teresa of Calcutta*

Texture was important in medieval eating because of the limited number of eating tools used. Most people carried a knife of the old, general-purpose dagger shape, and spoons were not uncommon. But the dinner fork was an oddity in most of Europe until the eighteenth century.
*Reay Tannahill, Food In History*

Bread is relief for all kinds of grief.
*Spanish Proverb*

One's stomach is one's internal environment.
*Samuel Butler*

Baking is not an art, it is an act of creation. This is not to say that the baker is an artist, for, again, baking is not an art. But in the act of creating a bread, an honest loaf, an object with a presence, a fragrance, a substance, a taste, some would say even a soul, the baker has changed grain and flour and

liquid into an entity. She or he has taken yeast, a dormant colony of living plants, and released and nurtured them in embryonic warmth, has sprinkled in sugar on which yeast thrives, has sifted in flour that builds the cellular elastic structure that holds the tiny carbon dioxide bubbles that raise the framework of the house called bread. And in that house is love, and warmth, and nourishment, and comfort, and care, and caring, and taking care, and time gone by, and time well spent, and things natural, and things good, and honest toil, and work without thought of reward, and all of those things once had, now lost in a country and a world that has rushed by itself and passed itself, running, and never noticed its loss.
*Yvonne Young Tarr, The New York Times Bread And Soup Cookbook*

Hors d'oeuvres have always a pathetic interest for me: they remind me of one's childhood that one goes through, wondering what the next course is going to be like—and during the rest of the menu one wishes one had eaten more of the hors d'oeuvres.
*Saki*

It is easy enough to read in statistical surveys, or even to say, that bread is to the Frenchman what rice is to the Chinese and what potatoes are to the Germans, and so on and on. Once a person has been exposed to the mystique of French bread, however, it is hard to class it with any other source of starchy nourishment.
*M. F. K. Fisher, The Cooking of Provincial France*

Bread is the Staff of Life, and while People have that, they need not give over Housekeeping.
*English Proverb, 16th Century*

The bigger the dairymaid,
the better the cheese.
*Derbyshire Proverb*

Spring, the sweet Spring, is the
year's pleasant king;
Then blooms each thing, then
maids dance in a ring,
Cold doth not sting, the pretty
birds do sing,
Cuckoo, jug, jug, pu we, to
witta woo.
The fields breathe sweet, the
daisies kiss our feet,
Young lovers meet, old wives
a-sunning sit,
In every street these tunes our
ears do greet,
Cuckoo, jug, jug, pu we, to witta
woo.
*Thomas Nashe, 1567–1602*

If we had no winter, the spring
would not be so pleasant: if we
did not sometimes taste of adversity, prosperity would not be
so welcome.
*Anne Bradstreet, c. 1612–1672*
*Thirty-three Meditations*

Meanwhile, until the world's
structure is held together by phil-
osophy, she [nature] maintains
its working through hunger and
through love.
*Friedrick Schiller*

The fagots blazed, the caldron's
smoke
Up through the green wood
curled;

# Cheese Soufflé

| | |
|---|---|
| 1 cup grated Parmesan or Romano cheese | 1 cup milk |
| 3 tablespoons margarine or butter | salt, pepper, nutmeg to taste |
| 3 tablespoons white flour or cornstarch | ½ lb. grated sharp cheddar cheese |
| | 6 eggs, separated |

Preheat oven to 375°. Liberally butter a 2-quart soufflé dish. Throw in Parmesan and coat whole dish. Prepare white sauce: melt margarine, add flour, stir till smooth, add milk. Stir till thickened. Add spice and seasonings. Add cheddar gradually and stir till smooth. (If too thick, add some milk.) Add beaten egg yolks to cheese sauce. Beat whites until very stiff. Fold into cooled cheese-yolk mixture; don't beat. Pour all into soufflé dish. Bake 30 minutes without opening oven. Serve hot as soon as it comes out.
    Serves 4.

*Spinach Soufflé*

Same as cheese soufflé, but add chopped cooked spinach (1 lb. fresh or frozen) and 1 sautéed onion to cheese-yolk mixture.

"Bring honey from the hollow
oak,
Bring milky sap," the brewers,
spoke,
In the childhood of the world.
*John Greenleaf Whittier*

The devils enter uninvited
when the house stands empty.
For other kinds of guests, you
have first to open the door.
*Dag Hammarskjöld, Markings*

Psychology has its Gresham's
Law; its bad money drives out the
good. Most people tend to perform the actions that require least
effort, to think the thoughts that
are easiest, to feel the emotions
that are most vulgarly commonplace, to give the rein to desires
that are most nearly animal.
*Aldous Huxley*

It has never ceased to be a source
of wonderment to me why a man
should prefer to chew pencils
when food that is far more wholesome and filling can be procured
at a trifling cost.
*Frank Sullivan*

My cheese, my digestion.
*William Shakespeare*

Some people want to see God
with their eyes as they see a cow,
and love Him as they love a cow
—for the milk and cheese and
profit it brings them.
*Meister Eckhart, 12th Century*

God of goodness, bless our food.
Keep us in a pleasant mood.
Bless the cook and all who serve
   us.
From indigestion, Lord, preserve
   us. Amen.
*Abbey Press Placemat*

Who never ate his bread with
   tears,
Who never sat weeping on his
   bed
During care-ridden nights
Knows you not, you heavenly
   powers.
*Goethe*

Fasting and feasting are universal
human responses, and any meal,
shared with love, can be an
*agape*.
*Elise Boulding*

Silence goes hand in hand with
fasting. Feasts demand sound
and music. There must be singing
and laughter.
*Jean-Paul Aron, The Art of Eating
in France*

Their best and most wholesome
feeding is upon one dish and no

# Creamy Cheese Toasts

(*Croque-monsieur*)

| | |
|---|---|
| 2 tablespoons butter | 2 eggs, separated |
| 2 tablespoons flour | 6 or 8 slices toast |
| 1 cup milk | |
| ¾ cup coarsely grated Swiss cheese | |

Melt butter; stir in flour; cook, stirring, about 3 minutes. Stir in milk. When sauce reaches boiling point, turn off heat. Stir in cheese. Beat egg whites until stiff; beat yolks until creamy. When sauce has cooled slightly, beat in the egg yolks, then the whites. *Chill thoroughly*. Spread generously on toast; place under broiler about 3 minutes, or until bubbly and browned.

The topping mixture can be made in advance and refrigerated. Then just spread on toast and pop into broiler for almost-instant lunch.

Serves 6 to 8.

more and the same plain and
simple: for surely this huddling
of many meats one upon another
of divers tastes is pestiferous. But
sundry sauces are more dangerous than that.
*Pliny*

A diet of food gives us bodily
health, a diet of people gives us
tranquillity of the soul.
*Bernardin de Saint-Pierre*

Many a man may use as simple a
diet as the animals, and yet retain
health and strength.
*Henry David Thoreau*

**The more faithfully you listen to
the voice within you, the better
you will hear what is sounding
outside. And only he who listens
can speak. Is this the starting
point of the road towards the
union of your two dreams—to be
allowed in clarity of mind to
mirror life and in purity of heart
to mold it?**
*Dag Hammarskjöld, Markings*

When the birds are teaching me I
hear Him.
*Brother Patrick Francis*

Cheese, that the table's closing
   rites denies,
And bids me with the unwilling
   chaplain rise.
*John Gay,
Trivia*

You have to ask children and birds how cherries and strawberries taste.
*Goethe*

What a large volume of adventures may be grasped within this little span of life, by him who interests his heart in everything, and who, having eyes to see what time and chance are perpetually holding out to him as he journeyeth on his way, misses nothing he can *fairly* lay his hands on!
*Laurence Sterne*

*Blessing of Grapes.* Bless, O Lord, this new fruit of the vine, which You were pleased to bring to maturity through the passing of the seasons, the drops of the rain, and propitious weather. Let it be a source of joy for those who shall partake of this offspring of the vine.
*A Prayer from the Eastern Catholic Church*

And I have felt
A presence that disturbs me with the joy
Of elevated thoughts; a sense sublime

# Raisin, Currant, or Blueberry Cake

½ cup butter or margarine, soft
1 cup sugar
2 eggs, separated
2 cups all-purpose flour
½ teaspoon salt
1 tablespoon double-acting baking powder

1 cup milk, at room temperature
1 teaspoon grated lemon rind
½ cup raisins, or fresh dried currants, or fresh blueberries

Preheat oven to 350°. Beat butter until smooth and fluffy. Beat in sugar, then 2 egg yolks, then flour, salt, and baking powder which have been sifted together; then add milk and lemon rind. Beat batter until very smooth and creamy. Add raisins (currants/blueberries). Beat egg whites stiff and fold into batter. Bake in greased 9-inch tube pan for about 40 minutes. Cool in pan. When cool, glaze if desired.

*Lemon Glaze:* (optional)

To the juice of 1 lemon, stir in confectioners sugar until desired consistency and sweetness. Spoon on cool cake; it will almost disappear into the cake.

Of something far more deeply interfused,
Whose dwelling is the light of setting suns,
And the round ocean and the living air,
And the blue sky, and in the mind of man:
A motion and a spirit, that impels
All thinking things, all objects of all thought
And rolls through all things.
*William Wordsworth*

I planted, Apollos watered, but God gave the growth.
*1 Corinthians 3:6,* RSV

On arrival at an early medieval house people washed their hands and dried them on a towel hung on the wall. Later it became customary for a servant to bring a basin and an ewer of warm water. The ewer was kept on its own 'ewery board'. The water in which people washed was specially prepared. You boiled up some sage, poured off the water, let it cool until tepid, then added camomile or marjoram or rosemary and boiled this with orange peel, perhaps adding a bay leaf or two.
*Katie Stewart, Cooking and Eating*

When you reap the harvest of your land, you shall not reap your field to its very border, neither shall you gather the gleanings after your harvest. And you shall not strip your vineyard bare, neither shall you gather the fallen grapes of your vineyard; you shall leave them for the poor and for the sojourner: I am the Lord your God. You shall not steal, nor deal falsely, nor lie to one another.

*Leviticus 19:9–1., The Radical Bible*

Man shall not live by bread alone, but by every word that proceeds from the mouth of God.

*Matthew 4:4, RSV*

*Bread and Soup.* These primeval foods became the earliest culinary comforts of primitive peoples. Soups brewed in caves and grains ground on stones and baked between glowing coals became the sustenance from which early civilization flowed. As long ago as yesterday and as near as tomorrow, bread and soup still sustain and comfort us. Here are our primary nutrients contained in golden loaves. Little wonder bread is called the staff of life . . . the representation of the body of Christ. For bread is good . . . as Life is good . . . as health is good. And soup is a simmering secret of vitamins and minerals

# Whole Wheat Bread

¾ cup honey and
¼ cup molasses
  (or 1 cup honey)
3 cups boiling water
1 cup cold water
3 packages dry yeast

¼ cup salad oil
10 cups whole wheat
  flour
1 tablespoon salt

Place honey and molasses in large bowl, add hot water, stir, add cold water. When liquid is lukewarm, sprinkle yeast evenly over mixture until yeast activates. Add salad oil, gradually add flour and salt. Knead on well-floured bread board until mixture is even. Place in greased bowl and cover with damp towel. Let rise 1 hour; knead; let rise again 45 minutes; knead. Place in well-greased bread loaf pans. Let rise 30 minutes. Bake at 350° about 30 minutes. Yields 3 loaves.

ready to nourish us and send us forth. It is probably safe to say that as soon as man (or was it woman?) invented the kettle, he or she promptly invented soup. For what easier, more delectable meal could the primitive gourmet concoct than a simmering caldron of bones and bits of meats, berries and roots, fern shoots and fruits, served with an elemental bread of ground wild grain mixed with water and baked on a hot, flat stone?

*Yvonne Young Tarr, The New York Times Bread And Soup Cookbook*

Let a good pound weight of

bread suffice for the day.
*Rule of St. Benedict*

I am God's wheat; may I be ground by the teeth of wild beasts that I may become the pure bread of Christ.
*Prayer of St. Ignatius of Antioch*

Music I heard with you was more than music,
And bread I broke with you was more than bread.
*Conrad Aiken*

*Blessing of Bread.* O Lord, Jesus Christ our God, You are the Bread of Angels and the Bread that gives eternal life. You came down from heaven for our sake and fed us with the spiritual food of your divine gifts. Look upon this bread, we humbly entreat You, and as You once blessed the five loaves in the wilderness, so now also bless this bread and those who partake of it.
*From a Monastic Ritual*

Animals feed themselves; men eat; but only wise men know the art of eating.
*Anthelme Brillat-Savarin*

One a penny, two a penny, hot
 cross buns;
If you have no daughters, give
 them to your sons.
*Mother Goose*

The future . . . seems to me no
unified dream but a mince pie,
long in the baking, never quite
done.
*E. B. White, One Man's Meat*

Live merrily as thou canst, for by
honest mirth we cure many pas-
sions of the mind. A gay companion is as a wagon to him that is
wearied by the way.
*Robert Burton*

He has spent his life best who has

# Basic Muffin Recipe

(*Gâteau Mentonnais*)

3 eggs
⅓ cup milk
2 cups whole wheat
 flour
¾ cup sugar

2 teaspoons baking
 powder
a pinch of salt
⅓ cup oil
2 tablespoons grated
 orange rind

Preheat oven to 350°. Grease muffin tins. Beat eggs
well; add milk. Beat in dry ingredients, oil, and orange
rind. Spoon into muffin tins, filling them about ⅓ full.
Bake about 45 minutes. Makes 12 muffins.

enjoyed it most. God will take
care that we do not enjoy it any
more than is good for us.
*Samuel Butler*

Drink because you are happy, but
never because you are miserable.
*G. K. Chesterton*

Happiness is made by the stomach.
*Voltaire*

Because of body's hunger are we
 born,
And by contriving hunger are we
 fed;

Because of hunger is our work
 well done,
As so are songs well sung, and
 things well said.
Desire and longing are the whips
 of God—
God save us all from death when
 we are fed.
*Anna Wickham*

It is life near the bone where it
is sweetest.
*Henry David Thoreau, Walden*

Many excellent cooks are spoiled
by going into the arts.
*Paul Gauguin*

To feed were best at home; from
thence the sauce to meat is
ceremony.
*William Shakespeare, Macbeth*

Better is a hard crust in thine
owne house, than a cram'd Capon
in another Mans.
*Mabbe*

Little Tom Tucker
Sings for his supper;
What shall he eat?
White bread and butter.
How will he cut it
Without e'er a knife?
How will he be married
Without e'er a wife?
*Mother Goose*

Marriage is our last, best chance
to grow up.
*Joseph Barth, Minister, King's Chapel,
Boston*

A good wife is the crown of
her husband.
*Proverbs 12:4,* RSV

Come. Holy Spirit, and enkindle in our hearts the fire of your love. Amen.

*Prayer for Pentecost*

The airs and streams renew their
  joyous tone;
The ants, the bees, the swallows
  reappear;
Fresh leaves and flowers deck the
  dead Season's bier;
The amorous birds now pair in
  every brake,
And build their mossy homes in
  field and brere;
And the green lizard, and the
  golden snake,
Like unimprisoned flames, out of
  their trance awake.

*Percy Bysshe Shelley, Adonais*

They feast on the riches of your
  house;
they drink from the stream of
  your delight.
In you is the source of life
and in your light we see light.

*Psalm 35:9, 10*

Sing with all the sons of glory,
Sing the resurrection song!
Death and sorrow, earth's dark
  story,
To the former days belong.

## Pentecost Cream

| | |
|---|---|
| ½ cup butter | 1 teaspoon vanilla |
| 1 quart milk | 1 package (10 to 12) |
| ½ cup flour | anisette spongecake |
| peel of ½ lemon, | fingers |
| sliced in thin strips | 2 cups sliced peaches |
| 4 whole eggs, well | ½ pint whipping cream |
| beaten with the sugar | ½ teaspoon brandy |
| ½ to ¾ cup sugar | ½ cup confectioners |
| ½ teaspoon anise | sugar |
| ¼ teaspoon nutmeg | tiny pinch nutmeg |

In a saucepan, melt butter; mix in milk, flour, lemon peel. Cook, stirring until it starts to thicken. Before it is boiling, stir in the sugar–egg mixture, and flavorings. When thickened, remove lemon peel. In a flat baking dish, alternate layers of this mixture with cake fingers and sliced peaches. End with a cake layer on top. Whip cream, brandy, confectioners sugar and nutmeg. Spread on top of cake layer. Chill 4–8 hours. Serves 8.

All around the clouds are break-
  ing,
Soon the storms of time shall
  cease;
In God's likeness, man awaking,
Knows the everlasting peace.

O what glory far exceeding
All that eye has yet perceived!
Holiest hearts for ages pleading,
Never that full joy conceived.
God has promised, Christ pre-
  pares it,
There on high our welcome waits;
Every humble spirit shares it,
Christ has passed th'eternal gates.

*William J. Irons, Sing with All the Sons of Glory, from The Methodist Hymnal*

My soul shall be filled as with a
  banquet,
my mouth shall praise you with
  joy.

*Psalm 62:6*

I eat to live, to serve and also,
it happens, to enjoy, but I do
not eat for the sake of enjoyment.

*Mohandas Gandhi*

The year's at the spring,
And day's at the morn;
Morning's at seven;
The hill-side's dew-pearl'd;
The lark's on the wing;
The snail's on the thorn;

God's in His heaven
All's right with the world!

*Robert Browning, Pippa's Song*

Every moment and every event of every man's life on earth plants something in his soul.

*Thomas Merton*

The only way to have more time, says Father Lacouture, "is to sow time." In other words, to throw it away. Just as one throws wheat into the ground to get more wheat.

*Dorothy Day*

Bad men live to eat and drink, Whereas good men eat and drink in order to live.

*Socrates*

# Pentecostal Cake

| | | | |
|---|---|---|---|
| ⅔ | cup scalded milk | 2 | egg whites |
| 1 | cup sugar | ¼ | teaspoon cream of tartar |
| 1⅓ | cups sifted flour | | |
| 3 | teaspoons baking powder | ¼ | teaspoon salt |
| | | 1 | teaspoon vanilla |

Scald milk and allow to cool. Sift sugar, flour, and baking powder together three times. Add scalded milk gradually, beating constantly. Add to egg whites cream of tartar, salt, and vanilla, and beat 1½ to 2 minutes, or until the egg whites refuse to slip when the bowl is tipped. Fold into floured mixture. Bake in an ungreased 7-inch tube pan at 350° for 45 minutes or until the cake is golden brown and firm to the touch. Invert the cake on a rack until cool.

Meanwhile, hull and clean 15 large strawberries. Crush 8 with a fork, and sweeten to suit. Make a frosting of 1½ cups of confectioners sugar, 2 tablespoons of soft butter or margarine, and 1½ tablespoons approximately of crushed strawberries in juice. Put the butter and sugar into a bowl, add crushed berries and juice, beating well with a fork. Add only enough to make a mixture of consistency to spread easily. Frost the cake and top with seven whole strawberries as a reminder of the gifts of the Holy Spirit.

Spring has now unwrapped the
  flowers,
Day is fast reviving,
Life in all her growing powers
Toward the light is striving;
All the world with beauty fill,
Gold and green enhancing;
Flowers make glee among the
  hills,
And set the meadows dancing.

Through each wonder of fair
  days
God himself expresses;
Beauty follows all his ways,
As the world he blesses;
So, as he renews the earth,

Artist without rival,
In his grace of glad new birth
We must seek revival.

Praise the Maker, all ye saints;
He with glory girt you,
He who skies and meadows
  paints
Fashioned all your virtue;
Praise him, seers, heroes, kings,
Heralds of perfection;
Brothers, praise him, for he
  brings
All to resurrection!
*Spring Has Now Unwrapped the
Flowers, from Methodist Hymnal*

A landscape can sing about God,
a body about Spirit.
*Dag Hammarskjöld, Markings*

A little Madness in the Spring
Is wholesome even for the King
*Emily Dickinson*

It is not growing like a tree
In bulk, doth make Man better
  be;
Or standing long an oak, three
  hundred year,
To fall a log at last, dry, bald,
  and sere:
A lily of a day
Is fairer far in May,
Although it fall and die that
  night—
It was the plant and flower of
  Light.
In small proportions we just
  beauties see;
And in short measures life may
  perfect be.
*Ben Jonson*

The Easter lily's dew-wet calyx.
Drops pausing
Between earth and sky
*Dag Hammarskjöld, Markings*

The field is God's table.
*Estonian Proverb*

And so throughout eternity
I forgive you, you forgive me;
As our dear Redeemer said,
This is the Wine, this is the
Bread.
*William Blake*

Now the green blade riseth from
the buried grain,
Wheat that in dark earth many
days has lain;
Love lives again, that with the
dead has been
Love is come again like wheat
that springeth green.

In the grave they laid him, Love
whom men had slain,
Thinking that never he would
wake again,
Laid in the earth like grain that
sleeps unseen:

# Easter Bread

| | |
|---|---|
| 2 cups milk, scalded | 2 eggs, well beaten |
| 1 package yeast | 1½ teaspoons salt |
| 6 cups flour | ½ cup raisins |
| 5 tablespoons shortening | ½ cup candied peel |
| | 1 teaspoon nutmeg |
| 1 cup sugar | 1 egg, slightly beaten |

Easter bread or Easter cake is baked in traditional ring molds and symbolizes eternity which has neither beginning nor end. Cool milk to lukewarm, dissolve yeast, add 2 cups of flour and beat well. Cream shortening with sugar, add eggs and beat well; add milk mixture with salt and remaining flour. Knead well; let rise in a warm place about 1½ hours. Work in remaining ingredients except for egg, and knead on floured board until dough does not stick. Place in a greased bowl, rub with butter, cover, and let rise until double in bulk. Knead again, and shape into 2 rings. Arrange them on a cookie sheet, brush over lightly with the beaten egg, and let rise until double again. Bake at 400° for 15 minutes, then reduce heat to 350° and bake for 15 minutes more. This recipe may be baked in 4 small loaves.

Love is come again like wheat
that springeth green.

Forth he came at Easter, like the
risen grain,
He that for three days in the
grave had lain;
Quick from the dead my risen
Lord is seen:
Love is come again like wheat
that springeth green.

When our hearts are wintry,
grieving, or in pain,
Thy touch can call us back to
life again,
Fields of our hearts that dead
and bare have been:
Love is come again like wheat
that springeth green.
*J. M. C. Crum, Now the Green Blade Riseth*

O Lord, teacher of wisdom and understanding. You are the instructor of the unwise and the defender of the poor. Strengthen and enlighten my heart, O Lord. Grant me to speak, O Word of God, and may my lips cry out to You: O Most Merciful One, have mercy on me, a sinful man.
*Lenten Prayer of the Sinner*

Be praised O my Lord by all
    Thy creatures
But chiefly by Brother Sun
Whom in the day Thou lighteneth
    for us
For fair is he and radiant with
    resplendence
And to Thee most high beareth
    the semblence.
*St. Francis of Assisi, Canticle of the
Sun*

What is man but a mass of
thawing clay?
*Henry David Thoreau, Walden*

The most precious, the most con-
soling, the most pure and holy,
the noble habit of doing nothing
at all.
*G. K. Chesterton*

O sons and daughters, let us sing!

The King of heaven, the glorious
    King,
O'er death today rose triumphing,
Alleluia! Alleluia!

That Easter morn at break of
    day,
The faithful women went their
    way

# Easter Spice Ring

| | |
|---|---|
| 3 tablespoons shortening | 1 teaspoon cinnamon |
| 1 cup sugar | 1 teaspoon each mace, nutmeg, and clove, mixed |
| 1 teaspoon baking soda | |
| 1 10¾ oz. can tomato soup | 1½ cups raisins or candied fruit-peel |
| 2 cups flour | |

Cream shortening and sugar. Stir soda into soup. Sift flour and spices and add to the mixture the creamed shortening and sugar. Stir well. Then add soup and raisins. Mix well. Bake in a 10–inch tube pan at 325° for 35 minutes. Remove from pan and allow to cool. Frost with the following:

*Orange Icing*

| | |
|---|---|
| 4 tablespoons soft margarine or butter | ¼ cup frozen orange juice concentrate, thawed |
| ¼ teaspoon salt | |
| ½ pound confectioners sugar | |

Cream butter, add salt, a little sugar and work together well. Add sugar and orange juice concentrate alternately in small portions, mixing thoroughly until icing spreads easily. When icing has set, arrange cake on a platter and insert into the hole in center a candle which has been melted slightly at the base to help it stand.

To seek the tomb where Jesus
    lay
Alleluia! Alleluia!

An angel clad in white they see,
Who sat and spake unto the
    three,
"Your Lord doth go to Galilee,"
Alleluia! Alleluia!

How blest are they who have not
    seen,
And yet whose faith hath con-
stant been;
For they eternal life shall win,
Alleluia! Alleluia!

On this most holy day of days,
Our hearts and voices, Lord we
    raise
To thee, in jubilee and praise,
Alleluia! Alleluia!
*Jean Tisserand, O Sons and
Daughters, Let Us Sing. French Carol
15th Century*

Who takes part in all feasts has
to suffer all hunger.
*Estonian Proverb*

O God, You dispel the darkness
of our life with the shining glory
of the Resurrection of Your Son.
Keep alive in the children of your
household the Spirit of Sonship
which You have poured upon
them, so that being renewed in
body and soul, they may serve
You with great purity of life,
through Christ our Lord. Amen.
*From the Easter Vigil*

Today is the beginning of our salvation,
and the revelation of the mystery
    planned from all eternity.
*Table Prayer for the Feast of the
Annunciation of the Lord, March 25*

Every day we are changing, every
day we are dying, and yet we
fancy ourselves eternal.
*St. Jerome*

# Summer

I'll tell you how the Sun rose
A Ribbon at a time
The Steeples swam in Amethyst
The news, like Squirrels, ran.
*Emily Dickinson*

One must summer and winter
with the land and wait its oc-
casions.
*Mary Austin, The Land of Little Rain*

Keeping time,
Keeping the rhythm in their
   dancing
As in their lives in one living
   season
*Eliot, Four Quartets*

Nature is not governed except by
obeying her.
*Francis Bacon*

A bowl of fresh, tender leaves
from any of half a hundred kinds
of garden lettuces, unadorned

# Watercress, Romaine Lettuce, and Fresh Mushroom Salad

| | |
|---|---|
| 1 tablespoon Dijon mustard (French preferable) | salt and pepper to taste |
| ¼ cup olive oil | ½ lb. fresh mushrooms |
| 2 tablespoons apple-cider vinegar | 1 bunch fresh watercress |
| 3 tablespoons chopped scallions | 1 bunch fresh romaine lettuce |

Place mustard and olive oil in a bowl and mix gradually with a wire whisk. When this is mixed well, add the vinegar, scallions, salt, and pepper and continue to beat and mix thoroughly. Clean and cut the stems from the mushrooms, slice thinly and mix with the dressing. Chill until ready to use.

Wash and rinse well both the watercress and the romaine lettuce. Cut and slice according to taste, but not very small. When ready to serve the salad, pour the dressing on watercress and lettuce and mix well.

Serves 8.

except by the simplest possible mixture of oil, vinegar and seasoning, is a joy to the palate.
*M. F. K. Fisher, The Cooking of Provincial France*

Beware of the devil—he hides in a sprig of parsley.
*A French Nun*

Salad and eggs, and lighter fare,
Tune the Italian spark's guitar.
*Matthew Prior*

If women but knew it, health is more apt to be maintained by what is done by them in the

kitchen than by what all the doctors and druggists can do for their families.
*Ralph Borsodi*

Mushrooms of one night be the best and they be little and red within and closed at the top; and they must be peeled and then washed in hot water and then parboiled and if you wish to put them in a pasty add oil, cheese and spice powder.
*The Goodman of Paris (Le Ménagier de Paris)*

What we need are more cooks, not more cookbooks.
*Tassajara Breadbook*

Eat well of the cresses.
*John Grange, The Golden Aphroditis*

Within every artichoke is an acanthus leaf, and the acanthus is what man would have made of the artichoke, had God asked him his advice.
*André Malraux*

The mind of the universe is communistic.
*Marcus Aurelius*

Peace is the nurse of Ceres, and Ceres is the foster-child of Peace.
*Ovid*

God, I can push the grass apart
And lay my finger on Thy heart!
*Edna St. Vincent Millay, Renascence*

Lettuce, like conversation, requires a good deal of oil, to avoid friction and keep the company smooth.
*Charles Dudley Warner, "Ninth Week," My Summer in a Garden (1871)*

He that drinks not wine after salad is in danger to be sick.
*English Proverb, 16th Century*

The poetry of earth is never
  dead:
When all the birds are faint with
  the hot sun,
And hide in cooling trees, a voice
  will run
From hedge about the new-mown
  mead;
That is the Grasshopper's—he
  takes the lead
In summer luxury—he has never
  done
With his delights; for when tired
  out with fun
He rests at ease beneath some
  pleasant weed.
The poetry of earth is ceasing
  never:
On a lone winter evening, when
  the frost
Has wrought a silence, from the
  stove there shrills
The Cricket's song, in warmth
  increasing ever,
And seems to one in drowsiness
  half lost,
The Grasshopper's among some
  grassy hills.
*John Keats, On the Grasshopper and
the Cricket*

Whatever befalls in accordance
with Nature should be accounted
good.
*Cicero*

For man, the vast marvel is to
be alive. . . . We ought to dance
with rapture that we should be
alive and in the flesh, and part
of the living, incarnate cosmos.
I am part of the sun as my eye
is part of me. That I am part of
the earth my feet know perfectly,
and my blood is part of the sea.

# Green and Beets Salad

1½ lbs. medium-sized
    beets
 1 head romaine lettuce
    *or* 1 bunch watercress
½ cup olive oil
 2 tablespoons cider-
    vinegar

½ teaspoon salt
½ teaspoon freshly
    ground pepper
 2 tablespoons chopped
    scallions
 1 tablespoon Dijon
    mustard

Cut the tops off beets. Put beets in a pan with boiling
water. Cook for about 1 hour or until tender. Drain
and cool, then peel, and cut into thin slices. Mix the
beets and the romaine lettuce and add oil, vinegar, salt,
pepper, scallions, mustard. Mix well and serve.
  Makes 6 servings.

My soul knows that I am part of
the human race, my soul is an
organic part of the great human
race, as my spirit is part of my
nation. In my own very self, I
am part of my family.
*Apocalypse*

Modern man . . . has come to
look upon nature as a thing outside himself—an object to be
manipulated or discarded at will.
It is his technology and its
vocabulary that makes his primary world. If, like the primitive,
he has a sacred center, it is here.
*Loren Eiseley*

Frugality and economy are virtues without which no household
can prosper. Whatever the in-
come, waste of all kinds should
be most sternly repressed . . .
Economy and frugality must
never, however, be allowed to
degenerate into meanness.
*Mrs. Beeton's Household Management*

Vocation is the spine of life.
*Friedrich Nietzsche*

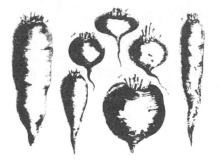

Let onion atoms dwell within the
  bowl,
And, scarce suspected, animate
  the whole.
*Sydney Smith, Recipe for
Salad Dressing*

Enough is as good as a feast.
*John Heywood*

I reckon—when i count at all
First—Poets—Then the Sun
Then Summer—Then the Hea-
ven of God
And then—The List is done.
*Emily Dickinson*

A single violet transplant
The strength, the colour, and the
size

## Vegetable-Cheese Casserole

2 medium (or 1 large) eggplants
3 cups milk
6 well-beaten eggs
2 teaspoons cornstarch
1 small onion, chopped
1 8 oz. package chopped frozen spinach, thawed and drained

salt, pepper, dash of nutmeg
bread slices seasoned with garlic salt and oregano
coarsely grated cheddar cheese

Slice and parboil eggplants. Mix all other ingredients except bread and cheese. Butter a large casserole dish. Fill with alternating layers of: milk mixture (on bottom), bread slices, milk mixture, cheese, eggplant slices, milk mixture. Repeat layers ending with milk mixture and cheese on top. Bake at 350° until heated through, about 1 hour.
    Serves 8.

(All which before was poor and scant)
Redoubles still, and multiplies.

When love with one another so
Interanimates two souls,
That abler soul, which thence doth flow,
Defects of loneliness controls.
*John Donne*

He who sings, prays twice.
*St. Augustine*

Peter Piper picked a peck of pickled peppers;
A peck of pickled peppers Peter Piper picked.

If Peter Piper picked a peck of pickled peppers,
Where's the peck of pickled peppers Peter Piper picked?
*Anonymous Nursery Rhymes*

In Good Queen Bess's day, the dockmen who unloaded cargoes of pepper wore uniforms without pockets as a measure against theft. During the reign of Henry II there was a pepper guild whose members were known as pepperers.
*Craig Claiborne, An Herb and Spice Cook Book*

For thousands of years man's culture lingered at this agricultural, civilizational level; but then in Great Britain toward the end of the eighteenth century, human culture took another quantum leap. The Industrial Revolution brought in a whole new technology, and with it a whole new art. The art was no longer a celebration of the glory of kings and princes, but the autobiography of the middle classes. It was a story of personal, individual movement in time and space: from rags to riches, from the country to the city and back again . . . Underneath the pursuit of wealth, power, and fame, and underneath the search for absolute autonomy, was the individual man confronting his solitude.
*William Irwin Thompson, Passages About Earth*

He only earns his freedom and existence who daily conquers them anew.
*Goethe*

Those who have drained the cup of joy in this world, will have a hangover in the other.
*Heinrich Heine*

If you will have the Hen's Egg; you must bear her Cackling.

*Dutch Proverb*

Vasari, in his *Lives of the Painters*, describes how Piero di Cosimo, finding that eating interfered with his work, took to living entirely on hard-boiled eggs. He cooked these a hundred at a time, and kept a basketful beside his easel. That is one way of simplifying the pursuit of beauty.

*Aubrey Menen*

Strange to see how a good dinner and feasting reconciles everybody.

*Samuel Pepys*

# Italian-Style Eggs with Noodles
*(Oeufs à l'italienne)*

½ lb. noodles
2 tablespoons butter
6 hard-boiled eggs
1 cup flavorful tomato sauce

½ cup grated Swiss cheese
bread crumbs

Preheat oven to 450°. Cook noodles; drain and toss with butter. Arrange around the edge of an oven-proof platter, leaving a hollow place in the middle. Cut the eggs into thick slices or lengthwise halves; place in the middle of the noodle ring. Pour tomato sauce over; sprinkle generously with grated cheese and bread crumbs. Bake 10 to 15 minutes, until cheese is bubbly and browned.

Serves 4 to 6.

It's always we ramble, that river and I,
All along your green valley I'll work till I die;
My land I'll defend with my life if needs be,
'Cause my Pastures of Plenty must always be free.

Woody Guthrie, *Pastures of Plenty
American Folksongs of Protest*

It is not enough to free man from the hunger imposed on him by an insufficiency of food. Man must be freed of all the forces that oppress him, of the natural, economic and political order.

*Youth delegates to the Second World Food Congress of the UNFAO, The Radical Bible*

What we give to the poor for Christ's sake is what we carry with us when we die.

*Peter Maurin*

It's a mighty hard row that my poor hands has hoed
And my poor feet has traveled a hot dusty road
Out of your dustbowl and westward we rolled,
Lord, your desert is hot and your mountains are cold.

I work in your orchards of peaches and prunes,
And I sleep on the ground 'neath the light of your moon.
On the edge of your city you'll see us and then
We come with the dust and we go with the wind.

California, Arizona, I make all your crops,
Then it's north up to Oregon to gather your hops;
Dig beets from your ground, cut the grapes from your vine
To set on your table your light sparkling wine.

Green Pastures of Plenty from dry desert ground,
From the Grand Coulee Dam where the waters run down;
Every state in this union us migrants has been
We'll work in your fight and we'll fight till we win.

Never does Nature say one thing and Wisdom another.
*Juvenal*

From the side of some hoar hill,
Through the high wood echoing
    shrill;
Sometime walking, not unseen,
By hedgerow elms, on hillocks
    green,
Right against the eastern gate,
Where the great sun begins his
    state,
Robed in flames and amber light,
The clouds in thousand liveries
    dight;
While the ploughman, near at
    hand,
Whistles o'er the furrowed land,
And the milkmaid singeth blithe,
And the mower whets his scythe,
And every shepherd tells his tale
Under the hawthorn in the dale.
Straight mine eye hath caught
    new pleasures,
Whilst the landskip round it
    measures.
Russet lawns and fallows gray,
Where the nibbling flocks do
    stray;
Mountains on whose barren
    breast
The laboring clouds do often rest;
Meadows trim, with daisies pied;
Shallow brooks and rivers wide.
*John Milton*

A scientific civilization in the full sense is an anomaly in world history. The civilizations of the sun never developed it. Only one culture, that of the West, has, through technology, reduced the religious mystique so long attached to agriculture. Never before have such large masses of people been so totally divorced from the land or the direct processing of their own foodstuffs.
*Loren Eiseley*

Mysticism keeps men sane.
*G. K. Chesterton*

# Spinach Casserole with Tomato Topping

3 cups medium white sauce (6 tablespoons butter, 6 tablespoons flour; stir until foamy, add 3 cups milk, 1½ teaspoons salt, ⅛ teaspoon pepper) dash of nutmeg
4 beaten eggs

1½ to 2 cups cubed stale whole wheat bread
2 8 oz. boxes frozen chopped spinach, thawed and drained or equivalent fresh spinach sliced cheddar cheese

Butter a casserole dish. Combine all above ingredients (except cheese) and place in dish. Cover with sliced cheese.

*Topping:*
2 or 3 fresh tomatoes
1 large onion, chopped

oregano, parsley, salt, pepper

Cut tomatoes into thick slices and fry briefly with chopped onion, oregano, parsley, salt, and pepper.
    Place tomato slices and seasonings on top of casserole. Bake at 350° until bubbly and browned, about 1 hour.
    Serves 6.

When it rains porridge the beggar has no spoon.
*Danish Proverb*

He that would have the fruit must climb the tree.
*Thomas Fuller, Gnomologia*

And recognizes ever and anon
The breeze of Nature stirring in
  his soul.
*William Wordsworth*

# Oatmeal and Fruit

| | |
|---|---|
| 1 tablespoon (approximately) oatmeal per person | a little water (optional) |
| pinch of salt | milk |
| sugar to taste | grated rind of an orange or a lemon |

The American and British custom of serving oatmeal for breakfast is little known on the continent. French and Italians who have "discovered" oatmeal use it most often for a light, hot supper dish. It is cooked with milk; a bit of fruit is added for taste, and it is delicious.

Mix the dry ingredients together and dilute in a little water or milk. Let stand 2 hours. Cook with the rind of orange or lemon. (There must be sufficient liquid to allow for the swelling of the oatmeal.) When it is cooked (1 to 5 minutes generally, depending on the variety of oatmeal used), add enough warm milk to make a more liquid mixture. (The quantity of milk added depends on taste. Some prefer the dish almost soupy; other like it firm.)

Another variant is to leave out the orange or lemon rind and serve the oatmeal and milk mixture with hot rhubarb which is cooked separately and added in tablespoonfuls as topping for the oatmeal.

Serves 3 or 4.

C——holds that a man cannot have a pure mind who refuses apple-dumpling. . . . Only I stick to asparagus which still seems to inspire gentle thoughts.
*Charles Lamb*

A barn in day, is a small night.
*John Updike*

Calm weather in June
Sets corn in tune.
*Mother Goose*

Our civilization still rests, and will continue to rest, on the discoveries made by peoples for the most part unknown to history. Historic man has added no plant or animal of major importance to the domestic forms on which he depends. He has learned lately to explain a good part of mechanisms of selection, but the arts thereof are immemorial and represent an achievement that merits our respect and attention. We remain a part of the organic world, and as we intervene more and more decisively to change the balance and nature of life, we have also more need to know, by retrospective study, the responsibilities and hazards of our present and our prospects as lords of creation.
*Carl O. Saver, Agricultural Origins and Dispersals*

One impulse from a vernal wood
May teach you more of man,
Of moral evil and of good,
Than all the sages can.
*William Wordsworth*

# Complete Meal
(*Repas complet*)

| | |
|---|---|
| 1  tablespoon (per person) uncooked oatmeal | Add: |
| | juice of 1 lemon |
| 1  apple (or any other fruit) per person, grated or cut fine | enough milk to make a moist, consistent mixture |
| a pinch of salt | ½  cup nuts |
| sugar to taste | 1  cup whipped cream |

This recipe provides a balanced, light meal. It can be prepared a day ahead and served when needed. (In Europe this would be for supper since the main meal is generally at noon. Americans would probably serve it for lunch.)

Combine all ingredients in the dish in which the meal will be served and mix well. Chill, and keep in the refrigerator. Any fruits can be used. Strawberries in season are particularly delicious. Use equivalent quantity of 1 apple per person, whatever the fruit(s) selected.

Ah dear nature, the mere remembrance, after a short forgetfulness, of the pine woods! I come to it as a hungry man to a crust of bread.
*Henry David Thoreau*

Beauty is a manifestation of secret natural laws, which otherwise would have been hidden from us forever.
*Goethe*

A sensitive approach to food may extend sensitivity almost without effort on our part, into other areas of our lives. Not only will our appreciation of the arts increase, but also we may be aided in practicing the most difficult and greatest art—that of friendly relationship to others. The art of getting along amicably with neighbors and friends requires true sensitivity, an awareness of all of man's hungers.
*Alan Hooker, Vegetarian Gourmet Cookery*

Nothing is so infectious as example, and we never do great good or evil without producing the like.
*La Rochefoucauld*

True universality does not consist in knowing much but in loving much.
*Jakob Burckhardt*

The trouble is, people do not work in peace and quiet. They bustle, like Martha.
*Dorothy Day*

All real works of art look as if they were done in joy.
*Robert Henri*

Mysticism has not the patience to wait for God's revelation.
*Sören Kierkegaard*

The meanest floweret of the vale,
The simplest note that swells the
gale,
The common sun, the air, the
skies,
To him are opening paradise.
*Thomas Gray, Ode on the Pleasure
Arising from Vicissitude*

# Creamed Mushrooms on Toast

(*Farce aux champignons*)

| | |
|---|---|
| ½ lb. mushrooms, washed and sliced | salt, pepper (garlic salt, optional) |
| 2 tablespoons butter and 1 tablespoon oil (for sautéing) | 4 tablespoons butter (for sauce) |
| | 4 tablespoons flour |
| ¼ cup diced onion or shallot | 2 cups milk |
| | 6 slices toast |

Sauté mushrooms until they begin to brown; add onion, salt, pepper (and optional garlic salt) and sauté gently until onion is transparent. Prepare a sauce with butter and flour and milk (melt butter, stir in flour; after flour has cooked 2 or 3 minutes, stir in milk; keep stirring until sauce comes to boil; season). Combine mushrooms and onions and sauce and spread on toast.

*Optional:* put under broiler to make the sauce bubbly and slightly brown on top.

Serves 6.

Man is to himself the most wonderful object in nature; for he cannot conceive what the body is, still less what the mind is, and least of all how a body should be united to a mind.
*Pascal*

Nature is a rag-merchant, who works up every shred and ort and end into new creations; like a good chemist whom I found, the other day, in his laboratory, converting his old shirts into pure white sugar.
*Ralph Waldo Emerson*

It is common knowledge that many modern products are adulterated, and it is therefore desireable that all housekeepers should be in a position to test the goods supplied to them. The following are some simple but effective tests.

*Coffee:* When purchasing ground coffee, gather a little in the palm of the hand and press firmly. If it sticks together in a ball, or cakes in lumps, it contains some adulterating substance. Pure coffee falls apart when the hand is opened.

*Mushrooms:* When cooking mushrooms, for safety's sake place a clean sixpence in the vessel in which they are being cooked. If the silver shows the least discoloration the mushrooms are unfit for human consumption.
*Mrs. Beeton's Household Management*

We are born believing. A man bears beliefs, as a tree bears apples.
*Ralph Waldo Emerson*

The swallows veering skimmed
the golden grain
At midday with a wing aslant
and limber;
And yellow cattle browsed upon
the plain.
*Trumbull Stickney, Mnemosyne*

# Corn Scallop

2 eggs, beaten
1 17-oz. can cream-
style corn
½ cup crushed soda
crackers
¼ cup undiluted evapor-
ated milk
¼ cup chopped green
pepper
1 teaspoon chopped
onion
½ teaspoon raw sugar

¼ cup butter or margar-
ine, melted
¼ cup finely shredded
carrot
1 tablespoon chopped
celery
6 drops tabasco
½ teaspoon salt
½ cup shredded cheddar
cheese
paprika

In large bowl, beat eggs with fork. Add the remaining ingredients (except cheese and paprika), and mix thoroughly. Put into a greased 8-inch square baking dish. Sprinkle with cheese and paprika. Bake at 350° for 30 minutes or until mixture is set and top is golden brown.

Adding some sesame seeds (about ¼ cup) gives a nice crunch.

About 8 servings, or dinner for 4.

Summer afternoon—summer afternoon; to me those have always been the two most beautiful words in the English language.
*Henry James, Quoted by Edith Wharton in A Backward Glance*

It seems as though I had not drunk from the cup of wisdom, but had fallen into it.
*Sören Kierkegaard*

So silent I when Love was by
He yawned, and turned away;
But Sorrow clings to my apron-
strings
I have so much to say.
*Dorothy Parker*

Make for the shortest path, which is that of nature; in other words, healthiness in every speech and action. For a man with this aim in life is free from all doubt and vexation, all thoughts of ways and means and all pretense.
*Marcus Aurelius*

Manners are like the cypher in arithmetic—they may not be much in themselves, but they are capable of adding a great deal to the value of everything else.
*Freya Stark*

Positively, the best thing a man can have to do is nothing, and, next to *that*, perhaps, good works.
*Charles Lamb*

Listen, now, verse should be as
  natural
As the small tuber that feeds on
  muck
And grows slowly from obtuse
  soil
To the white flower of immortal
  beauty.
*R. S. Thomas*

The most instructive experiences
are those of everyday life.
*Friedrich Nietzsche*

# Cloister Carrots

6 or 8 large carrots
1 quart milk (or use the powered milk equivalent)
1 cup raisins
½ cup blanched, slivered almonds
2 tablespoons brown sugar

Wash and scrape the carrots; cut in very thin slices. Pour the milk in a pot, add carrots, raisins, almonds, and the brown sugar. Bring to boil and then simmer for 1 hour, stirring occasionally. Serve hot in the winter, or chill and serve cold in the summer.
  Makes 6 to 8 servings.

Love your life, poor as it is. You may perhaps have some pleasant, thrilling, glorious hours, even in a poorhouse. The setting sun is reflected from the windows of the almshouse as brightly as from the rich man's abode.
*Henry David Thoreau, Walden*

Busy, curious, thirsty fly!
Drink with me and drink as I:
Freely welcome to my cup,
Couldst thou sip and sip it up:
Make the most of life you may,
Life is short and wears away.
*William Oldys,*
*On a Fly Drinking*
*Out of His Cup*

The joy of life is to put out one's power in some natural and useful or harmless way. There is no other. And the real misery is not to do this.
*Oliver Wendell Holmes*

God accepteth the good will and the labour of his servants, no matter how we feel.
*Julian of Norwich, 13th century Anchoress*

As one has to learn to read or to practice a trade, so one must learn to feel in all things, first and almost solely, the obedience of the universe to God. It is really an apprenticeship, it requires time and effort.
*Simone Weil, Waiting For God*

Knowledge rests not upon truth alone, but on error also.
*C. G. Jung*

We must not forget that the literal translation of the word "asceticism" is "training exercise." The monks took it over from the sport vocabulary of the Greek athletes.
*José Ortega y Gasset*

Nature was actually as well read as an alphabet; it was the real "tool" by which man survived with a paucity of practical equipment.
*Loren Eiseley*

There is nothing better for a man than that he should eat and drink, and find enjoyment in his toil. This also, I saw, is from the hand of God.

*Ecclesiastes 2:24, RSV*

In cooking with herbs and spices the eye and the nose are nearly as important as a knowing palate. It is virtually impossible to judge the relative age and quality of a dried herb or spice in the home kitchen except by sight and smell. The greener the herb, such as tarragon, or the redder the spice, such as paprika, the more likely that it has retained its best flavor traits.

*Craig Claiborne, An Herb And Spice Cook Book*

Tree at my window, window tree, My sash is lowered when night
  comes on;

# Sautéed Zucchini

| | |
|---|---|
| 4 medium-sized zucchinis | 2 tablespoons chopped parsley |
| ½ cup oil, or butter if preferred | salt and fresh pepper |
| 2 tablespoons chopped scallions or shallots | |

Wash zucchinis and cut into sticks without peeling the skin or removing the seeds. Place in boiling salted water for 5 minutes. Drain. Just before serving, pour the oil (olive oil if possible) or melt the butter in a pan and add the zucchini immediately. Add chopped scallions and parsley, and salt and pepper according to taste. Sauté 5 minutes and serve when warm and tender.

    Makes 6 servings.

But let there never be curtain
  drawn
Between you and me.

*Robert Frost*

Moonlight is sculpture.

*Nathaniel Hawthorne*

Beauty is a mystery. You can neither eat it nor make flannel out of it.

*D. H. Lawrence*

To waste, to destroy, our natural resources, to skin and exhaust the land instead of using it so as to increase its usefulness, will result in undermining in the days of our children the very prosperity which we ought by right to hand down to them amplified and developed.

*Theodore Roosevelt, Message to Congress, December 3, 1907*

Earth is here so kind, that just tickle her with a hoe and she laughs with a harvest.

*Douglas Jerrold, A Land of Plenty*

The earth has enough for every-man's need but not for every man's greed.

*Mahatma Gandhi*

In America, in our frenzied efforts to take advantage of high prices for agricultural products, we are mining our soils instead of farming them.

*Joseph A. Cocannouer*

Eat with the rich, but go to the play with the poor, who are capable of joy.

*Logan Pearsall Smith, Afterthoughts*

How can an unhappy hen lay a good egg?

*Joe Nichols*

Well may we labour, still to dress This garden, still to tend plant, herb, and flower.

*John Milton*

By the labour of your hands you shall eat.

*Psalm 127:2, RSV*

# Cheese Sauce

1 cup cold milk
2 tablespoons of flour
2 tablespoons of butter
salt, pepper

⅓ to ½ cup any cheese cut into small chunks or cottage cheese

In saucepan combine all ingredients except cheese. Heat to boiling over medium heat, stirring constantly. Boil and stir one minute. Add cheese. Can be poured over macaroni, brown rice, cauliflower, broccoli, potatoes, etc. The sauce can also be used in a casserole with layers of wheat germ. (Wheat germ adds protein and makes casserole thick.)

Makes 1 cup.

ing cannot be hastened. If the preparations for dinner have been somewhat delayed, nothing is gained by placing the saucepan on the top of a fierce fire. When once the slow-boiling or simmering point has been reached all excess of heat is wasted, and the benefit of slow progressive cooking is lost.
*Mrs. Beeton's Household Management*

Art is the demonstration that the ordinary is extraordinary.
*Amédée Ozenfant*

Where's the cook? is supper ready, the house
trimmed, rushes strewed, cobwebs swept?
*William Shakespeare, Taming of the Shrew*

No worldly thing
Can a continuance have
Unless love back again it bring
Unto the cause which first the essence gave.
*Boethius, Philosophiae Consolationis*

One must work, nothing but work. And one must have patience.
*Auguste Rodin*

Whatever the manner in which we earn our daily bread, we become mentally exhausted at the shop or store, or office, from the many problems we have to try to solve and the tensions we have to endure. What a rest and relaxation, on arrival home, to change into our old patched clothes and step out into a quiet, happily growing garden.
*J. I. Rodale*

In Homeric times, even kings were not above cooking their own meals, and, judging by the pictures of kitchens scenes and the models found in the tombs, the Egyptian cooks were all men,

as were Greek and Roman cooks.
*Katie Stewart, Cooking and Eating*

One day Isabel de Santo Domingo found Teresa in front of the kitchen stove in ecstasy: "Dear God! our Mother [Teresa] will upset the little oil that's left us on the fire!" Teresa did not loosen her grip of the handle of the frying pan one whit and the eggs went on sizzling. . . . She was Martha and Mary in one.
*St. Teresa of Avila, Marcelle Auclair*

The inexperienced cook should take this lesson to heart—cook-

# Spanish Tuna

| | |
|---|---|
| ¼ cup oil | 1 no. 2 can tomatoes |
| 1 cup rice | ½ cup tomato juice |
| 1 medium onion, sliced thin | 1 cup water |
| ⅓ cup chopped green pepper | 2 cans (4 oz. each) sliced mushrooms with liquid |
| 1 teaspoon salt dash of cayenne | 1 7-oz. can chunk-style tuna, drained and flaked |
| 1 clove garlic | |

Heat oil in saucepan or large skillet. Add rice. Sauté
until golden. Add onions, green pepper, salt, cayenne,
garlic clove, tomatoes, tomato juice, water, and un-
drained mushrooms. Cook, covered, over low heat 35
to 40 minutes or until rice is done, stirring occasionally.
Add tuna. Cover and heat through.
    Serves 4.

Fish . . . never doth digest well . . . except it swimme twice after it comes forth the water: that is, first in butter, so to be eaten: then in wine or beere after it is eaten.
*West. for Smelts*

Everything living forms an atmosphere around itself.
*Goethe*

We who lived in concentration camps can remember the men who walked through the huts comforting others, giving away their last piece of bread. They may have been few in number, but they offer sufficient proof that everything can be taken away from a man but one thing: the last of the human freedoms—to choose one's attitude in any given set of circumstances, to choose one's own way.
*Victor Frankl*

Among primitive peoples it would seem that cooking has always been the woman's job; but as soon as people became civilized and began to think of what they ate as a gift from the gods for which they should be grateful, a

## Scalloped Fish

| | | |
|---|---|---|
| 1½ | lbs. fish fillets | salt, pepper to taste |
| 1 | 10¾-oz. can mushroom soup | dash Worcestershire sauce |
| 2 | tablespoons green pepper, diced | 4 slices bread, lightly toasted and cubed |
| 1 | can green peas, drained | ¼ cup melted butter or substitute |
| ¼ | cup lemon juice | |

Dice fish fillets into ½-inch cubes. Mix all ingredients (except bread crumbs and butter); place in well-greased baking dish. Cover with bread crumbs which have been mixed with melted butter, or sprinkle with grated preferred cheese. Bake at 350° until heated through and brown on top (about 1 hour).
Serves 4.

religious element entered into the preparation of food which then seems to have become the duty of men. And so it seems to have been with cooking, certainly where the preparation of the 'burned offerings', were concerned—those token sacrifices which purported to give the gods their 'share' of the food, but which were mere whiffs of glorious smells, while their priests and the people ate the food.
*Katie Stewart, Cooking and Eating*

Many housekeepers, in lieu of doing a large amount of cooking

each day, now have a "cooking morning," two or three times a week; on these days they do as much as possible of the cooking likely to be needed on the following couple of days. By this means, for a day or two after a "cooking morning," little will be required save heating up, and plenty of time will be found for necessary "odd jobs," which should be carefully listed and so arranged as to fit in with the daily routine.
*Mrs. Beeton's Household Management*

But what is your duty? The demands of every day.
*Goethe*

To what a cumbersome unwieldiness
And burdenous corpulence my love had grown
But that I did, to make it less
And keep it in proportion,
Give it a diet, made it feed upon
That which love worst endures,
*discretion*
**John Donne**

"A loaf of bread," the Walrus
    said,
"Is what we chiefly need:
Pepper and vinegar besides
Are very good indeed—
Now, if you're ready, Oysters
    dear,
We can begin to feed."
*Lewis Carroll, Alice in Wonderland*

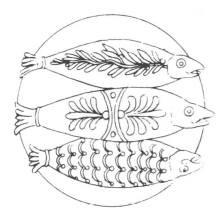

Therefore, if food is a cause of
my brother's falling, I will never
eat meat, lest I cause my brother
to fall.
*I Corinthians 8:13,* RSV

*Blessing of New Fruits.* We thank
You, O God, and we offer You
the first fruits which You have

# Stuffed Fish
(*Farce au poisson*)

½ lb. fish fillets
4 to 6 slices bread, diced
    small amount milk
1 egg, slightly beaten
    dash of nutmeg

salt, pepper
parsley
basil or dill
4 large tomatoes

Preheat oven to 350°. Chop fish. Soak bread in milk
(amount determined by dryness of bread) and egg.
Combine with fish and seasonings. Cut top off tomatoes
and hollow them out. Stuff with fish mixture and bake
in a greased dish for 45 minutes, until fish is cooked.

This is an excellent way to use leftover fish. Baking
time will be shorter in that case—30 minutes.

Stuffing can also be baked and then used to stuff
deviled eggs, crêpes, and so on.

Serves 4.

one who is hungry, nor anger a
man in want. Do not add to the
troubles of an angry mind, nor
delay your gift to a beggar. Do
not reject an afflicted suppliant,
nor turn your face away from the
poor. Do not avert your eye from
the needy, nor give a man occasion to curse you; for if in bitter-
ness of soul he calls down a curse
upon you, his Creator will hear
his prayer.
*Ecclesiasticus 4:1–6* RSV

Etiquette means behaving yourself a little better than is absolutely essential.
*Will Cuppy*

Love is anterior to life,
Posterior to death,
Initial of creation, and
The exponent of breath.
*Emily Dickinson*

When a man's stomach is full, it
makes no difference whether he
is rich or poor.
*Euripides*

No act of kindness, no matter
how small, is ever wasted.
*Aesop, The Lion and the Mouse*

given us to enjoy and have produced by your word, bidding the
earth to bring forth all kinds of
fruits to refresh and feed mankind and all the beasts.
*From the Apostolic Constitutions of
the Early Church*

I would rather make mistakes in
kindness and compassion than
work miracles in unkindness and
hardness.
*Mother Teresa of Calcutta*

My son, deprive not the poor of
his living, and do not keep needy
eyes waiting. So not grieve the

A thing of beauty is a joy for
    ever:
Its loveliness increases; it will
    never
Pass into nothingness; but still
    will keep
A bower quiet for us, and a sleep
Full of sweet dreams, and health,
    and quiet breathing.
*John Keats, A Thing of Beauty*

The life of the soul is truth and
the awareness of the soul is love.
*St. Bernard of Clairvaux*

Even crumbs are bread.
*Danish Proverb*

# Egg Croquettes
(*Croquettes d'oeufs*)

2 tablespoons butter
2 tablespoons flour
1 cup milk
2 eggs, separated

6 hard-boiled eggs, diced
bread crumbs, seasoned
(parsley, salt, pepper,
onion salt)
oil for cooking

Prepare a white sauce with the butter, flour, and milk. Stir in the egg yolks and let cool. Stir in the diced eggs. Beat the egg whites until stiff. Form the cooled egg mixture into 1-inch balls. Roll in the egg white, then in the bread crumbs. Fry in heated oil until browned on all sides.

Serves 4.

It is a strange fact, but not the less true, that to get a well-made omelet in a private house in this country is the exception and not the rule. A few general remarks on making omelets will, we hope, not be out of place in writing a book on an exceptional style of cookery, in which omelets should play a most important part.

First of all, we require an omelet-pan. The best omelet-pan of all is a copper one, tinned inside. It is very essential that the frying-pan be absolutely clean, and it will be found almost essential to reserve the omelet-pan for omelets only.

The great question is, how much butter should be allowed for, say,

six eggs? On this point the greatest authorities differ. We will first quote our authorities, and then attempt to give an explanation that reconciles the difference. A plain omelet may be roughly described as settings of eggs well beaten up by stirring them up in hot butter. One of the oldest cookery books we can call to mind is entitled "The Experienced English Housekeeper," by Elizabeth Raffald. The book, which was published in 1775, is dedicated to the Hon. Lady Elizabeth Warburton, whom the authoress formerly served as housekeeper. The recipe is entitled "To make an amulet." The book states, "Put a quarter of a pound of butter into a frying pan, break six eggs." Francatelli also gives four ounces of butter to six eggs.

On the other hand, Soyer, the great cook, gives two ounces of butter to six eggs; so also does the equally great Louis Eustache Ude, cook to Louis XVI.

We may add that "Cassell's Dictionary of Cookery" recommended two ounces of butter to six eggs, whilst "Cassell's Shilling Cookery" recommends four eggs.

The probable reason why two such undoubtedly great authorities as Soyer and Francatelli should differ is that in making one kind of omelet you would use less butter than in making another. Francatelli wrote for what may be described as that "high class cooking suited for Pall Mall clubs," where no one better than himself knew how best to raise the jaded appetite of a wealthy epicure. Soyer's book was written for the people.

In Holland, Belgium, and Germany, and in country villages in France, the omelet is made, as a rule, with six eggs to two ounces of butter. In the higher-class restaurants in Paris, like Bignon's, or the Cafe Anglais, the omelet is lighter, and probably about four ounces of butter would be used to six eggs.

This probably explains the different directions given in various cookery books for making omelets.

*A. G. Payne, B.A., Cassell's Vegetarian Cookery, 1891*

# Spinach Pancakes

*Make a crêpe batter:*

| | |
|---|---|
| 2 eggs | 1 cup milk |
| 1 cup flour | |

Let batter sit in refrigerator while you prepare filling.

*Filling:*

3 tablespoons butter
1 chopped onion
2 cloves garlic, minced
1 bunch fresh spinach, washed and chopped (or 1 8-oz. box frozen, thawed and chopped)
4 hard-boiled eggs, chopped

1 cup coarsely grated cheddar cheese
1½ cups cream sauce (3 tablespoons butter, 3 tablespoons flour, 1½ cups milk, dash nutmeg, salt, pepper)

In a nonaluminum pan (aluminum tends to blacken spinach and/or make it taste bitter, acidy), melt butter; gently sauté (don't brown) the onion. Add garlic, stir, then add chopped spinach. If fresh spinach is used, cover for about 2 minutes to wilt it down. Turn off heat. Make thin crêpes. In each one put spinach, egg, cheese; roll up and place in baking dish. When all rolls are in, cover with cream sauce. Bake at 300° for 15 minutes.
Serves 4 to 6.

On looking at the archaic Apollo, Rilke said to himself: "Du musst Dein Leben ändern"—"You must make your life over." So it is on looking at Apollo 17. For those astronauts who have looked on the earth from space, the command has been literally taken to heart as they felt their consciousness being transformed to behold God making all thing new. Perhaps this transformation of consciousness, this new aesthetic high in man's culture, is the strongest argument in favor of manned space flight.
*William Irwin Thompson, Passages About Earth*

Be praised O my Lord by Brother
Wind
By air, and cloud and sky and
every clime
To whom Thou giveth sustenance
unto their kind
*St. Francis of Assisi, Canticle of the Sun*

My soul can find no staircase to Heaven unless it be through Earth's loveliness.
*Michelangelo*

By a small sample we may judge of the whole piece.
*Cervantes, Don Quixote*

## Apple Tapioca

½ cup minute or instant tapioca (scant ½ cup)

1 teaspoon salt (scant teaspoon)

1 cup sugar, brown or white (amount depends on tartness of apples)

2 teaspoons lemon juice

3 cups water

3 cups apples, pared, cored, and sliced (applesauce may be used)

dash of cinnamon cloves, allspice (optional)

In saucepan, combine tapioca, salt, sugar, lemon juice. Mix with water. Bring to a boil over medium heat, stirring constantly. Pour over apples in a baking dish. Spices may be sprinkled on top of apples. Cover and bake at 325° until apples are tender, approximately 45 minutes.

Serves 6.

A humble knowledge of oneself is a surer road to God than a deep searching of the sciences.
*Thomas a Kempis*

The discovery of a new dish does more for the happiness of mankind than the discovery of a star.
*Anthelme Brillat-Savarin, Psychologie du Goût*

The Lord my pasture shall
    prepare,
And feed me with a shepherd's
    care;
His presence shall my wants
    supply,
And guard me with a watchful
    eye.
*Joseph Addison, The Spectator*

In his theological science fiction novel *Out of the Silent Planet*, C. S. Lewis describes the surprise of the first space voyager who discovers that space is not a void, but a divine plenum. Men are prisoners of war in an enemy territory that shuts out all the vibrations of heaven, but all those who break out of this, the devil's planet soon regain their cosmic orientation.
*William Irwin Thompson, Passages About Earth*

I have seen the apples there that
    toss you secrets—
Beloved apples of seasonal madness
That feed your inquiries with
    aerial wine.

Put them again beside a pitcher
    with a knife,
And poise them full and ready for
    explosion—
The apples, Bill, the apples!
*Hart Crane, Sunday Morning Apples*

If you find yourself really ill, send for a good physician. Have nothing to do with quacks; and do not tamper with quack medicines. You do not know what they are; and what security have you that they know what they are?
*Mrs. Child, The American Frugal Housewife*

Hunger is not only the best cook, but also the best physician.
*Peter Altenberg*

Men do not have to cook their food; they do so for symbolic reasons to show they are men and not beasts.
*Edmund Leach*

All those who are contented with this life pass like a shadow and a dream, or wither like the flower of the field.
*Cervantes*

From every point on earth we are equally near to heaven and to the infinite.
*Frédéric Amiel*

## Apple Bath

*(This is the literal translation of the French and Italian names of this dish!)*

| | |
|---|---|
| 2 eggs, lightly beaten, just enough to blend thoroughly | 1 teaspoon flour |
| | 1 grated lemon peel |
| | a little milk |
| ½ teaspoon salt | 2 apples |

Mix eggs, salt, flour, lemon. Add just enough milk to make more liquid. The mixture should not be too dry. Add the apples, grated or cut very thin. Let stand for 3 hours. Fill a large frying pan with about ¾ inches of good cooking oil. Drop in tablespoonfuls of the batter and cook until crusty. Sprinkle with sugar and, if desired, cinnamon. Serve in a covered dish to keep hot.

Adam was but human—this explains it all. He did not want the apple for the apple's sake, he wanted it only because it was forbidden.

*Mark Twain, Pudd'nhead Wilson*

Timid roach, why be so shy?
We are brothers, thou and I.
In the midnight, like thyself,
I explore the pantry shelf!

*Christopher Morley, Nursery Rhymes for the Tender-Hearted*

If hunger makes you irritable, better eat and be pleasant.

*Sefer Hasidim*

This I conceive to be the chemical function of humor: to change the character of our thought.

*Lin Yutang*

It is now and in *this world* that we must live.

*André Gide*

Father, all-powerful and ever-living God, today we rejoice in the holy men and women of every time and place. May their prayers bring us your forgiveness and love. Through Christ, our Lord. Amen.

*From the Roman Missal, Feast of All Saints*

To him a little meant sufficiency.

*Chaucer, Canterbury Tales*

The only certainties that don't break down are those acquired in prayer.

*Reinhold Schneider*

If a man does not keep pace with his companions, perhaps it is because he hears a different drummer. Let him step to the music which he hears, however measured or far away.

*Henry David Thoreau, Walden*

For the Christian who loves God, worship is the daily bread of patience.

*Honoré de Balzac*

Heaven is to her the place where
  painters go,
All who bring beauty on frail
  shell or horn,
There was all made, thence their
  lux-mundi drawn,
Drawn, drawn, till the thread is
  resilient steel,
Lost though it seems in darken-
  ing periods,
And there they return to do
  work that is God's.
So this old lady writes, and
  again I believe,
I believe it all, and for no man's
  death I grieve.

*Derek Walcott, A Letter from Brooklyn*

Music fathoms the sky.

*Charles Baudelaire*

By the fruites and not by flowers, we do know the good tree.
*English Proverb, 16th Century*

Life eternal! heaven rejoices:
Jesus lives who once was dead;
Join, O man, the deathless voices;
Child of God, lift up thy head!
Partriarchs from the distant ages,
Saints all longing for their
    heaven,

# Apple Roll

2½  cups chopped peeled
    apples
½   teaspoon cinnamon

2   cups corn syrup
    juice of ½ lemon
    (optional)

*Shortcake:*

2   cups flour
1   teaspoon salt
1   tablespoon plus 1
    teaspoon baking
    powder

6   tablespoons shorten-
    ing
½   cup water

Preheat oven to 450°. Heat syrup to boiling, then keep ready in an 8-inch square baking pan. Work flour, shortening, and other ingredients like pastry; add water. Roll out dough to ⅓-inch thickness in a narrow oblong (approximately 12 inches long, 6 to 8 inches wide). Sprinkle apples, cinnamon, and optional lemon over dough. Roll up and pinch edges to seal. Cut into slices about 1½ inches wide. Immediately place slices, cut edge down, in boiling syrup. Bake for about 25 minutes. Spoon syrup over cakes and serve warm.

Prophets, psalmists, seers, and
    sages,
All await the glory given.

Life eternal! O what wonders
Crowd on faith; what joy un-
    known,
When, amidst earth's closing
    thunders,
Saints shall stand before the
    throne!
O to enter that bright portal,
See that flowing firmament,
Know, with thee, O God im-
    mortal,
"Jesus Christ whom thou hast
    sent!" Amen.
*William J. Irons, Sing with All the Sons of Glory, from The Methodist Hymnal*

Man draws the nearer to God as he withdraws further from the consolations of the world.
*Thomas a Kempis*

You crown the year with your
    goodness.
Abundance flows in your steps,
in the pastures of the wilderness
    it flows.
*Psalm 64:12*

In eating, a third of the stomach should be filled with food, a third with drink, and the rest left empty.
*Talmud*

A poem should be palpable and
   mute
As a globed fruit.
*Archibald MacLeish*

Crusts may be dried in the oven
and used for crumbing. Sippets
for soup can be made by baking
stale bread in the oven, and there
are numerous puddings which
have bread and breadcrumbs as
ingredients.
*Mrs. Beeton's Household Management*

Their tables were stored full, to
glad the sight, And not so much
to feed on as delight.
*William Shakespeare, Pericles*

If it happens that you are well
off, in your heart be tranquil
about it—if you can be just as
glad and willing for the opposite
condition. So let it be with food,
friends, kindred, or anything else

# Apple Crumble

| | |
|---|---|
| 1 quart apples, cut as for pie | 1 teaspoon baking powder |
| 1 cup flour | ¼ teaspoon salt |
| ½ cup sugar | 1 egg, unbeaten |

Fill 9-inch round cake pan with apples. Mix all other
ingredients until crumbly and sprinkle over apples.
Sprinkle top with melted butter or substitute. In 375°
oven, bake 30 minutes or until apples are done.
   Serves 6.

that God gives or takes away.
*Meister Eckhart*

Fasting is more effective than
charity, for the latter is done
with money, the former with
one's person.
*Berakot, Talmud*

When you reap the harvest of
your land, you shall not reap
your field to its very border,
neither shall you gather the
gleanings after your harvest.
And you shall not strip your
vineyard bare, neither shall
you gather the fallen grapes of

your vineyard; you shall leave
them for the poor and for the
sojourner.
*Leviticus 19:9,* RSV

Civilized man . . . is engaged
primarily with his deepening shell
of technology which either ex-
ploits the natural world or thrusts
it aside.
*Loren Eiseley*

Have you ever watched children
swinging? in order to lift themselves higher . . . they have to
dig their toes into the earth.
*Opatoshu, In Polish Woods*

I do not fear God, because I love
Him, and love casts fear out of
doors.
*St. Anthony the Great, The Father of Monks*

What the sick man likes to eat
is his medicine.
*Russian Proverb*

Knowst thou the land where the
   lemon trees bloom,
Where the gold orange glows
   in the deep thicket's gloom,
Where a wind ever soft from the
   blue heaven blows,
And the groves are of laurel and
   myrtle and rose?
*Goethe*

# Yogurt Cake

3  cups sifted flour
2  cups sugar
1  teaspoon baking
   powder (double if
   whole-wheat flour is
   used)

3  eggs
1  cup natural yogurt*
1  teaspoon vanilla
¾  cup oil

Preheat oven to 350°. Butter and flour an 8-inch square
cake pan. Combine dry ingredients. Beat eggs thoroughly. Beat in yogurt, vanilla, oil, dry ingredients.
Pour into baking pan. Bake about 50 minutes.

* Avoid yogurts containing "stabilizers" and other artifice. If you can
get natural yogurt with fruits, etc., they will work fine; decrease sugar if
yogurt is sweetened.

May the road rise with you
And the wind be ever at your
   back
And may the Lord hold you in
   the hollow of His hand.
*Gaelic Blessing*

Own only what you can always
carry with you: know languages,
know countries, know people. Let
your memory be your travel bag.
*Alexander Solzhenitsyn*

We shape our dwellings, and
afterwards our dwellings shape
us.
*Winston Churchill*

Training is everything. The
peach was once a bitter almond;
cauliflower is nothing but cabbage with a college education.
*Mark Twain, Pudd'nhead Wilson*

There should be less talk; a
preaching point is not a meeting
point.
*Mother Teresa of Calcutta*

A little in the morning, nothing
at noon, and a light supper doth
make to live long.
*Anonymous*

The loves of some people are but
the results of good suppers.
*Nicolas Chamfort*

A riddle, a riddle,
As I suppose;
A hundred eyes,
And never a nose.
*Mother Goose*

By all means use sometimes to
   be alone.
Salute thyself: see what thy soul
   doth wear.
Dare to look in thy chest, for 'tis
   thine own:
And tumble up and down what
   thou find'st there.
*George Herbert*

Bread on a journey is no burden
*Russian Proverb*

It is part of a woman's life to be preoccupied with food.
*Dorothy Day*

Several monastic orders, the Bernardine especially, made a profession of good living. Cooks employed by the cloth surpassed the limits of their own art; and when Monsieur de Pressigny (who died archbishop of Besançon) returned from the conclave which elected Pius VI in 1775, he said that the best dinner offered to him in all Rome was at the table of the head of the Capuchins.
*Anthelme Brillat-Savarin*

Not a wine-bibber, not a glutton.
*Rule of St. Benedict, A Description of a Monk*

There is no love sincerer than the love of food
*George Bernard Shaw*

A crack in the jug? Then you have let it get cold.
*Dag Hammarskjöld, Markings*

Marry, sir, 'tis an ill cook that cannot lick his own fingers.
*William Shakespeare*

# Butterless, Milkless, Eggless Cake

Boil together in a saucepan (*cooked mixture*).

| | |
|---|---|
| 1 cup brown sugar | ½ teaspoon nutmeg |
| 1¼ cups hot water | ½ teaspoon cloves |
| ⅓ cup shortening | 1½ teaspoons allspice |
| ⅔ cup raisins | |

Mix in a small bowl (*cold mixture*):

| | |
|---|---|
| 1 teaspoon soda | 2 cups sifted flour |
| 1 teaspoon salt | 1½ teaspoons baking powder |
| 2 tablespoons cold water | |

Add the cold mixture to the cooked mixture after it has cooled. Gradually stir in flour and baking powder. Mix thoroughly. Turn into a well-greased, floured 8-inch square pan. Bake at 325° for about 50 minutes.

To lengthen thy life, lessen thy meals.
*Benjamin Franklin, Poor Richard's Almanack*

Being happy is a virtue too.
*Ludwig Börne*

In seventy or eighty years, a man may have a deep gust of the world; know what it is, what it can afford, and what 'tis to have been a man.
*Samuel Taylor Coleridge*

Alleluia—O give thanks to the Lord for He is good,

for His love endures for ever. Give thanks to the God of gods, for His love endures for ever. Give thanks to the Lord of lords, for His love endures for ever.
*Psalm 135:1–3*

The tree that God plants no wind hurts it.
*English Proverb*

Behold, what I have seen to be good and to be fitting is to eat and drink and find enjoyment in all the toil with which one toils under the sun the few days of his life which God has given him, for this is his lot.
*Ecclesiastes 5:18,* RSV

Who fills your life with good things, renewing your youth like an eagle's.
*Psalm 102:5*

Who built Thebes of the Seven
  Gates?
In the books stand the names
  of Kings.
Did they then drag up the rock-
  slabs?

The young Alexander conquered
  India.
He alone?
Caesar beat the Gauls.
Without even a cook?

A victory on every page
Who cooked the victory feast?

*Bertolt Brecht*

# Butterless, Milkless, Eggless Chocolate Cake

| | |
|---|---|
| 1⅛ cups shortening | 2¼ teaspoons baking |
| 3⅜ cups sugar | powder |
| 1⅛ cups cocoa | 1¾ teaspoons salt |
| 3 cups hot water | 1½ teaspoons cinnamon |
| 2¼ teaspoons baking | 1½ teaspoons nutmeg |
| soda | 2¼ tablespoons vinegar |
| 5¼ cups flour | 2¼ teaspoons vanilla |

Cream shortening and sugar, add cocoa mixed with ½
the water, and soda in the other ½. Add flour mixed
with baking powder, salt, nutmeg, and cinnamon. Add
vinegar and vanilla. Bake in greased floured 8–inch pan
at 350° for 45 to 50 minutes.

O Lord Jesus Christ our God,
You blessed the five loaves and
with them You fed five thousand:
Do the same, O Lord, with this
food and drink, multiply them in
this room and throughout the
world; and sanctify all the faithful who shall partake of them.
Amen.

*A Byzantine Blessing*

One feast, one house, one mutual
happiness.

*William Shakespeare, Two Gentlemen
of Verona*

The vocation of a monk obliges
him to live separated from the
world but he finds himself at the
very heart of that which is most
intimate in each of his fellow
men; he is in living communion
with the essential aspirations
which God has placed like seeds
in his creature. The reason for
the monk's being is identified
with the reason for being that is
in every man.

*A Carthusian Monk*

When you place yourself at table,
listen quietly and without dis-
turbance to what is read according to the custom, until you rise;
so that not your mouth alone
may receive food, but your ears
also may nourish themselves with
the word of God.

*Rules of the Institute of St. Augustine
for the Sisters*

Youth is a continual intoxication;
it is the fever of reason.

*La Rochefoucauld*

To sleep easy all night,
Let your supper be light,
Or else you'll complain
Of a stomach in pain.

*Mother Goose*

Pat-a-cake, pat-a-cake, baker's man,
Bake me a cake as fast as you can;
Pat it and prick it, and mark it with B,
Put it in the oven for baby and me.
*Mother Goose*

A parent must respect the spiritual person of his child, and approach it with reverence.
*George Macdonald*

How inimitably graceful children are in general—before they learn to dance.
*Samuel Taylor Coleridge*

. . . Dance is the only art of which we ourselves are the stuff of which it is made.
*Ted Shawn*

For everything that lives is holy, life delights in life.
*William Blake*

There is a great man who makes every man feel small. But the real

# Vianney Buns

Take some bread dough (dark or white), flatten to ½ or ¾ inch, and with biscuit cutter, cut out rounds. Press scraps together to form irregular buns. Let the dough rise to twice the bulk. Place on papered (or greased) tray in 370–400° oven and bake for 20 minutes until they are "not quite burnt."

great man is the man who makes every man feel great.
*G. K. Chesterton*

They dined on mince, and slices of quince,
Which they ate with a runcible spoon;
And hand in hand, on the edge of the sand,
They danced by the light of the moon.
*Edward Lear*

Man is the only animal that laughs and weeps; for he is the only animal that is struck with the difference between what things are, and what they ought to be.
*William Hazlitt*

The important events in the world are not deliberately brought about; they simply happen.
*G. C. Lichtenberg*

Whoever absorbs a work of art into himself goes through the same process as the artist who produced it—only he reverses the order of the process and increases its speed.
*Friedrich Hebbel*

# Granola

| | |
|---|---|
| 4 cups rolled oats | ½ to 1 cup chopped almonds |
| 3 handfuls sunflower seeds | 2 to 3 tablespoons good oil |
| 1 handful sesame seeds | 2 to 3 tablespoons honey |
| 1 handful cocoanut | |
| ½ handful wheat germ | |

Mix all ingredients and spread out in pan in oven. "Bake" at 350°–375° for ½ hour or so until it is crisp and crunchy but not burned! Watch last 10 minutes or so, for it will burn rather suddenly. Serve with lots of milk and honey.

*Alternate:* "bake" only oatmeal and add other dry ingredients after.

Makes about 8 cups.

The staple dish of these first Romans was *puls*, or *pulmentum*. It was a kind of mush made from grain—in those days usually millet or spelt, a primitive type of wheat, and sometimes chick-pea flour. To this day the modern version of *pulmentum*, called *polenta*, can be eaten in either version—soft (and heated), with about the consistency of mashed potatoes, or hard (and usually cold), when it can be sliced like cake.
*M. F. K. Fisher, The Cooking of Provincial France*

# Autumn

## Lentil and Lemon-Peel Soup

1 cup lentils, washed  
1 quart water (perhaps more)  
peel of ½ lemon, grated  

1 onion, finely chopped  
garlic salt (optional)  
salt, pepper  

Combine all ingredients, and boil until lentils are tender. Check often to make sure there is enough water.

Serves 6.

I heard an Angel singing  
When the day was springing:  
'Mercy, Pity, Peace  
Is the world's release.'

Thus he sang all day  
Over the new-mown hay,  
Till the sun went down,  
And haycocks looked brown.  
*William Blake*

Is it an earthquake or simply a  
    shock?  
Is it the good turtle soup or  
    merely the mock?  
*Cole Porter, At Long Last Love*

September blow soft  
Till the fruit's in the loft.  
*Mother Goose*

Now doesn't it seem reasonable  
that it is better to eat life than

death? The firsthand protein of live, fresh, raw fruits and vegetables and nuts rather than the secondhand protein of dead, rapidly decaying flesh?  
*Dick Gregory, Dick Gregory's Natural Diet for Folks Who Eat: Cookin' with Mother Nature*

I'll make you feed on berries and on roots, And feed on curds and whey.  
*William Shakespeare, Titus Andronicus*

It was in the fifth century that fine cooking came to Athens from Sicily along with Sicilian

cooks, who were all men. Good chefs were choosey and many wanted to see a list of the guests before accepting an engagement. Good quality and simplicity seem to have been the main characteristic, plus those qualities that come from slow cooking.  
*Katie Stewart, Cooking and Eating*

Who will eat the kernel of the nut must break the shell.  
*John Grange, The Golden Aphroditis*

Indeed, the growth of the garden is symbolic of the growth of the soul. The proper environment

must be created, weeds that might choke out the finer, more delicate qualities of the soul must be removed, and all actions must be guided by the love that fulfills all laws.  
*The Findhorn Community, The Findhorn Garden*

Season of mists and mellow fruit-  
    fulness,  
Close bosom-friend of the matur-  
    ing sun:  
Conspiring with him how to load  
    and bless  
With fruit the vines that round  
    the thatch-eves run;  
To bend with apples the mossed  
    cottage-trees,  
And fill all fruit with ripeness to  
    the core;  
To swell the gourd, and plump  
    the hazel shells  
With a sweet kernel; to set bud-  
    ding more,  
And still more, later flowers for  
    the bees,  
Until they think warm days will  
    never cease,  
For Summer has o'er-brimmed  
    their clammy cells.  
*John Keats, To Autumn*

'Tis the voice of the Lobster: I
    heard him declare
'You have baked me too brown, I
    must sugar my hair.'
*Lewis Carroll, Alice in Wonderland*

One sage has noted that if the
onion were not quite so common
it would be the most coveted of
vegetables. It is probably true
since it may be the groundwork
for flavoring more main dishes
than any other single ingredient
barring butter, salt and pepper.
*Craig Claiborne*

Let first the onion flourish there,
Rose among roots, the maiden-
    fair
Wine-scented and poetic soul
Of the capacious salad bowl.
*Robert Louis Stevenson*

# Fish Chowder

| | |
|---|---|
| 2 large onions, finely chopped | 2 lbs. flaked fish |
| 8 large potatoes, peeled and cubed | 1½ quarts milk<br>salt |

Sauté onions in butter, add potatoes with a little bit of
water, and cook together. Steam fish separately, then
add onions, potatoes and fish to previously heated milk,
together with all cooking liquids. Add salt, simmer
chowder briefly, and serve.
    Serves 8.

Nobody can write the life of a
man, but those who have eat and
drunk and lived in social inter-
course with him.
*Samuel Johnson, from Boswell's Life
of Johnson*

Be praised O my Lord by Sister
    Water
For useful is she, lowly, precious
    and chaste.
*St. Francis of Assisi, Canticle of the
Sun*

To the bird's young ones he gives
food.
*Corneille*

For the man who would eat like
    a glutton,
A good stomach is worth more
    than mutton,
For what use is the best,
If you cannot digest,
And your teeth are exceedingly
    rotten?
*Leon de Fos, Gastronomia*

The fasts . . . shall be to the
house of Judah seasons of joy
and gladness, and cheerful feasts.
*Zechariah 8:19*

In the evening of life we shall be
judged on love.
*St. John of the Cross*

Beauty does not make the pot
boil.
*Irish Proverb*

If you bear the cross unwillingly,
you make it a burden, and load
yourself more heavily; but you
must needs bear it. If you cast
away one cross, you will certainly
find another, and perhaps a heav-
ier.
*Thomas a Kempis*

Eat nothing that will prevent you
from eating.
*Ibn Tibbon, Tzavaah, c. 1190*

The squirrel gloats on his accom-
    plish'd hoard,
The ants have brimm'd their
    garners with ripe grain,
And honey bees have stored
The sweets of Summer in their
    luscious cells;
The swallows all have wing'd
    across the main;
But here the autumn Melancholy
    dwells,
And sighs her tearful spells
Amongst the sunless shadows of
    the plain.
*Thomas Hood, Autumn*

# Garden Cottage Cheese

¼ cup chopped green
peppers
¼ cup chopped celery
2 tablespoons chopped
chives or onions

2 tablespoons chopped
olives, green or black
2 cups cottage cheese

Mix all ingredients and serve on lettuce leaves for a
high protein luncheon or salad.
     Serves 4.

Most people eat as though they
were fattening themselves for the
market.
*E. W. Howe*

No matter what conditions
Dyspeptic come to feaze,
The best of all physicians
Is Apple-pie and cheese!
*Eugene Field*

More people are killed by over-
eating and drinking than by the
sword.
*Sir William Osler*

If you wish to grow thinner, di-
  minish your dinner,
And take to light claret instead
  of pale ale;

Look down with an utter con-
  tempt upon butter,
And never touch bread till it's
  toasted—or stale.
*H. S. Leigh, A Day for Wishing*

He knew that to offer a man
friendship when love is in his
heart is like giving a loaf of
bread to one who is dying of
thirst.
*Margaret Wolfe Hungerford, The
Jessamy Bride*

There is strong shadow where
there is much light.
*Goethe*

Lord, grant that I may seek
  rather
To comfort, than to be com-
  forted.
To understand, than to be under-
  stood.
To love, rather than to be loved.
For it is by giving
That one receives.
It is by forgiving
That one is forgiven.
*Prayer of St. Francis of Asissi*

Treat the other man's faith
gently; it is all he has to believe
with. His mind was created for his
own thoughts, not yours or mine.
*Henry S. Haskins*

A hungry stomach has no ears.
*La Fontaine*

If we seek God, He will appear to
us: and if we hold Him, He will
stay with us.
*Abbot Arsenius*

The fact is that my native land
is a prey to barbarism, that in it
men's only God is their belly,
that they live only for the present,
and that the richer a man is the
holier he is held to be.
*St. Jerome*

The business of life is to go forward.
*Samuel Johnson*

For he on honey-dew hath fed,
And drunk the milk of Paradise.
*Samuel Taylor Coleridge*

Everything must have in it a sharp seasoning of truth.
*St. Jerome*

Aside from these culinary virtues, there is sheer poetry in the very names of herbs and spices that are commonly called on to contribute countless nuances in the world of food. Savory, sorrel, basil and clove, saffron, sage and more by the score. . . .
*Craig Claiborne, An Herb And Spice Cook Book*

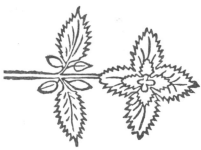

Fuelless cookery has undergone a revival, and it has became a general practice in some households, the revival having no doubt been influenced by the increased cost of fuel, the simplicity of the process, and motives of general economy.
*Mrs. Beeton's Household Management*

# Lentil Salad

*Combine:*

| | |
|---|---|
| 2 cups chilled boiled lentils | 1 cup grated carrots |
| 1 onion, finely chopped | ½ cup chopped radishes |

*Dressing:*

| | |
|---|---|
| ¼ cup vinegar | salt, pepper |
| ½ cup oil | garlic salt |

Serves 6 to 8.

There is no other door to knowledge than the door nature opens; there is no truth except the truths we discover in nature.
*Luther Burbank*

"Lord, if you helped a little more, more people would follow you!" But God does not listen to such entreaty . . . Right there, halfway along our road, we don't know whether we are going backwards or forwards.
*Carlo Carretto, Letters from the Desert*

I dwell in Possibility
A fairer House than Prose
More numerous of Windows
Superior—for Doors.
*Emily Dickinson*

An unturned vat awaits with
      ancient wine,
Within my house. Come quickly!
      Lose no time!
*Horace*

The peach will have wine, the fig water.
*English Proverb*

What is food to one man may be fierce poison to others.
*Lucretius*

Happy the man who far from schemes of business, like the early generations of mankind, works his ancestral acres with oxen of his own breeding, from all usury free.
*Horace*

The mountain and the squirrel
Had a quarrel;
And the former called the latter
  "Little Prig."
Bun replied,
"You are doubtless very big;
But all sorts of things and
  weather
Must be taken in together
To make up a year

# Woodchuck

| | | | |
|---|---|---|---|
| 2 | green peppers, chopped | 1 | 2-oz. jar pimentos, cut up |
| 1 | lb. mushrooms, sliced | | salt to taste |
| ½ | lb. butter or margarine | 9 | hard-cooked eggs, sliced |
| 2 | cups milk | | baking powder biscuits |
| 5 | tablespoons flour | | |
| ½ | lb. mild cheddar cheese, cut up | | |

Sauté green peppers and mushrooms in butter until tender. In a double boiler, cook and stir milk, flour, and cheese to thick white sauce consistency. Add sautéed vegetables and pimentos. Season. Fold in sliced eggs. Heat through. Serve over hot biscuits.
  Serves 8.

And a sphere.
And I think it's no disgrace
To occupy my place.
If I'm not so large as you,
You are not so small as I,
And not half so spry.
I'll not deny you make
A very pretty squirrel track;
Talents differ: all is well and
  wisely put;
If I cannot carry forests on my
  back,
Neither can you crack a nut."
*Ralph Waldo Emerson, Fable*

God gives the nuts, but he does not crack them.
*German Proverb*

You give but little when you give of your possessions. It is when you give of yourself that you truly give.
*Kahlil Gibran, The Prophet*

This only is charity, to do all, all that we can.
*John Donne*

A fat paunch never breeds fine thoughts.
*Greek proverb*

Our struggle is not easy. Those who oppose our cause are rich and powerful, and they have many allies in high places. We are poor. Our allies are few. But we have something the rich do not own. We have our own bodies and spirits and the justice of our cause as our weapons.
*Cesar Chavez*

A man's work whether in music, painting or literature is always a portrait of himself.
*Samuel Butler*

Nature, the vicar of th' almighty Lord.
*Geoffrey Chaucer*

O Heavenly King, the Consoler,
  the Spirit of Truth,
Who are everywhere and fill all
  things.
Treasury of blessings, and giver
  of life.
Come and dwell in us.
Cleanse us from every sin,
and save our souls, O Good One!
*From the Eastern Church*

There's no sauce in the world like hunger.
*Cervantes, Don Quixote*

If, my Torquatus, you can kindly
   deign
To lie on beds of simple form,
   and plain,
And sup on herbs alone, but
   richly dress'd,
At evening I expect you for my
   guest.
*Horace*

The stomach carries the feet.
*Irish Proverb*

An indigestion is an excellent
commonplace for two people that
never met before.
*William Hazlitt*

There is a Southern proverb—
fine words butter no parsnips.
*Sir Walter Scott, The Legend of
Montrose*

Hunger is the handmaid of genius.
*Mark Twain*

The name curry derives from a
Hindustani work, turcarri, col-

# Spicy Rice-Vegetable Casserole

Heat slowly together, to prevent burning (stir often):

| | |
|---|---|
| 3 tablespoons butter | 1 onion, chopped |
| ½ green pepper, chopped | 2 cloves garlic, mashed |
| | 1½ cups rice (uncooked) |

Slice and stir into mixture:

| | |
|---|---|
| 3 carrots | 3 large stalks celery |

Season with:

| | |
|---|---|
| ½ teaspoon thyme | salt, pepper |
| ½ teaspoon oregano (adjust to your taste) | |

Pour on 3½ cups boiling water. Stir thoroughly. *Cover*.
Bake at 350° for 1 hour.
   *Variation:* Stir in 1 cup warmed Mexican chick-
peas (garbanzos) when rice is cooked.
   Serves 6 to 8.

loquially shortened in India to
turri. This was corrupted slightly
to be pronounced curry in English. Curry powder is a blend of,
generally, ten or more spices. In
India, where the curry originated,

the word means sauce, and
several curries, each of them with
different flavours, may be served
during the course of one meal.
The color of most curry powders
is derived from the goldenrod
yellow of turmeric.
*Craig Claiborne, An Herb And
Spice Cook Book*

The meeting of two personalities
is like the contact of two chemical
substances: if there is any re-
action, both are transformed.
*Carl Jung*

Eden is that old-fashioned House
We dwell in every day
Without suspecting our abode
Until we drive away.
*Emily Dickinson*

He who receives his friends, and
takes no personal care in preparing the meal that is designed for
them, is not deserving of friends.
*Anthelme Brillat-Savarin*

The desert of the monk is his
monastery—and his own heart.
Yet in that desert he is free to
encounter and love the whole
world.
*Thomas Merton*

Frugality and good husbandry makes things go far; in great incomes.
*English Proverb, 16th Century*

The test of our progress is not whether we add more to the abundance of those who have much; it is whether we provide enough for those who have too little.
*Franklin D. Roosevelt, Second Inaugural Address, January 20, 1937*

Part of the secret of success in life is to eat what you like and let the food fight it out inside.
*Mark Twain*

Loving-kindness is the better part of goodness.
*W. Somerset Maugham*

The charges we bring against

# Poor Person's Sukiyaki

| | |
|---|---|
| 1 cup scallions or onions finely sliced | sugar to taste, if desired |
| ½ cup light cooking sherry or sweet wine | soy bean curd (tofu) cut in squares (if available) |
| ½ cup soy sauce | |
| 2 cups fresh spinach or well-drained frozen (any steamed greens can be substituted) mushrooms, if available other vegetables can be added | 4 cups cooked or 1½ cups uncooked rice (or any combination of rice and beans such as blackeye peas and rice, pinto beans and rice, etc.) |

Cook scallions or onions according to "pseudosautéing method" (see p.124). Add sherry and soy sauce and stir. Add spinach and other vegetables. Simmer 3 or 4 minutes. Add a little sugar as sauce cooks, if desired. Remove from heat. Add tofu and pour mixture over rice or rice and bean combination.

Other vegetables can be added. Amounts of all ingredients can be varied.

Serves 6 to 8.

others often come home to ourselves; we inveigh against faults which are as much ours as theirs; and so our eloquence ends by telling against ourselves.
*St. Jerome*

It is only by feeling your love that the poor will forgive you for the gifts of bread.
*St. Vincent de Paul*

Whom the heart of man shuts out,
Sometimes the heart of God takes in.
*J. R. Lowell*

It was a common saying among the Puritans, "Brown bread and the Gospel is good fare."
*Mathew Henry, Commentaries*

Chew well with your teeth and you'll feel it in your toes.
*R. Meir, Talmud*

The fattest belly is sensitive to pain and, indeed, few things can be more difficult to bear than the indigestion of the rich.
*Eric Gill*

The gray-green stretch of sandy
  grass,
Indefinitely desolate.
A sea of lead, a sky of slate;
Already autumn in the air, alas!
One stark monotony of stone,
The long hotel, acutely white,
Against the after-sunset light
Withers gray-green, and takes
  the grass's tone.
*Arthur Symons, Color Studies.
At Dieppe*

# Tomatoes Stuffed with Mushrooms

(*Farce aux champignons*)

| | | | |
|---|---|---|---|
| ¼ | lb. mushrooms | 1 | egg, beaten slightly |
| 1 | cup water | 1 | tablespoon chopped |
| 4 | slices bread, diced | | parsley |
| ½ | cup diced onion | | salt, pepper |
| 2 | tablespoons butter | 6 | tomatoes |

Wash mushrooms thoroughly and cut up. Cook 5 minutes in 1 cup boiling water. Remove from water and put the bread in to soak up all the water. Gently sauté the onions in the butter until transparent. In a bowl, beat the egg, parsley, seasonings. Add mushrooms, bread, onions, and mix thoroughly. Stuff into hollowed-out tomatoes which are then baked for 15 minutes.
  Serves 6.

One ought, every day at least, to hear a little song, read a good poem, see a fine picture, and, if it were possible, to speak a few reasonable words.
*Goethe*

For the "society" which is the family lives beautifully by its own spontaneous inner laws. Love is the rule.
*Thomas Merton*

God never tied man's salvation to any pattern. Whatever possibilities inhere in any pattern of life inhere in all, because God has given it so and denied it to none. One good way does not conflict with another.
*Meister Eckhart*

He who marries is like the doge who marries the Adriatic—he doesn't know what's in it: treasures, pearls, monsters, unknown storms.
 *Heinrich Heine*

One should believe in marriage as in the immortality of the soul.
*Honoré de Balzac*

In love it is enough to please each other by lovable qualities and attractions; but to be happy in marriage it is necessary to love each other's faults, or at least to adjust to them.
*Nicolas Chamfort*

Where God is merry, there write
  down thy fears:
What He with laughter speaks,
  hear thou with tears.
*Robert Herrick, God's Mirth, Man's Mourning*

Between man and wife even thoughts are contagious.
*Friedrich Nietzsche*

He that speaks, sows, and he that holds his peace, gathers.
*English Proverb*

Being young is beautiful, but being old is comfortable.
*Ebner-Eschenbach*

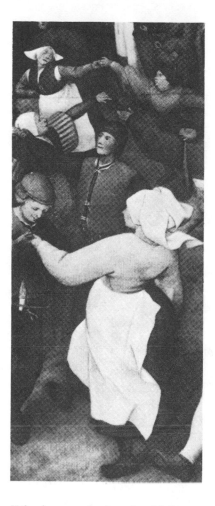

Who has good wine should flagon
   it out
And thrust the bad where the
   fungus sprout;
Then must merry companions
   shout:
This song wants drink!

When I see wine into the clear
   glass slip
How I long to be matched with it;
My heart sings gay at the thought
   of it:
This song wants drink!

I thirst for a sup; come circle the
   cup:
This song wants drink!
*This Song Wants To Drink, 12th*
*Century French Song*

# Risotto
(*Seasoned rice*)

| | |
|---|---|
| 1 onion | small handful) rice |
| 1 carrot | per person |
| 2 stalks celery | salt to taste |
| small quantity oil for | 2 cups any broth or |
| sautéing | bouillon |
| 1½ tablespoons (or 1 | ½ cup white wine |

In a large frying pan, gently sauté finely chopped onion, carrot, and celery in a little good cooking oil. Add rice sufficient for the number of servings desired. (The other ingredients listed are for approximately 6 persons. For much larger servings, they should all be proportionately augmented.)

Mix all ingredients except wine well and season. Cook over medium heat. When the mixture begins to stick to the pan, add the wine. Continue cooking long enough to cook the rice. The mixture will dry out as it cooks, so keep adding a little bouillon to maintain moistness. If the rice is a variety which cooks quickly, you may have some bouillon left over. If, however, you use brown rice or another longer-cooking variety, you may have to add more broth or bouillon. Stir only to prevent sticking and when adding liquid. Otherwise let it simmer gently.

Serve in a covered bowl which has been warmed. At the last minute sprinkle with grated cheese (Parmesan is best).

Serves 6.

We often feel sad in the presence of music without words; and often more than that in the presence of music without music.
*Mark Twain*

Life was meant to be lived, and curiosity must be kept alive. One must never, for whatever reason, turn one's back on life.
*Eleanor Roosevelt*

A man who lives in indifference is one who has never seen the woman he could love.
*Jean de La Bruyère*

The sum which two married people owe to one another defies calculation. It is an infinite debt, which can only be discharged through all eternity.
*Goethe*

Seldom, or perhaps never, does a marriage develop into an individual relationship smoothly and without crises; there is no coming to consciousness without pain.
*Carl Jung*

It is not lack of love but lack of friendship that makes unhappy marriages.
*Friedrich Nietzsche*

May your laughter be from God.
*Irish Proverb*

Hunger is a good seasoning for any dish.
*Gentili, Mleket Mahshebet, Noah, 1710*

The world can get along without pepper, not without salt.
*Johanan. TJ: Horayot 3.5*

The quality of life within [the Findhorn] community can be likened to a greenhouse environment where the growth and transformation of each individual is stepped up.
*The Findhorn Community, The Findhorn Garden*

The vegetable world presents no less variety to our nourishment, no fewer resources.
*Anthelme Brillat-Savarin*

Whatsoever was the father of the disease, an ill diet was the mother.
*George Herbert*

Hunger teaches a man many things.
*Irish Proverb*

# Indian Curried Lentils

*Boil:*

| | |
|---|---|
| 1 pound lentils | a few peppercorns |
| 1 quarts of water (perhaps more) | 1 cinnamon stick |

Drain lentils. Remove peppercorns and cinnamon stick.

*Just before serving, add the following sauce:*

| | |
|---|---|
| 2 good-sized onions, sliced | 3½ cups canned whole tomatoes |
| margarine | salt to taste. |
| 1 tablespoon or more curry powder | |

Sauté onions in margarine and then add the other ingredients. Stir and heat through. Two quartered hard-boiled eggs or an equivalent number of shrimp may also be added.
Serves 4.

What, sir, would the people of the earth be without woman? They would be scarce, sir, almighty scarce.
*Mark Twain*

We have always known that heedless self-interest was bad morals; we know now that it is bad economics.
*Franklin D. Roosevelt, Second Inaugural Address, January 20, 1937*

Man and woman function reciprocally and are so delicately related that each feels the effects of the other's failure. Man was created male and female, two distinct and correlative creatures, each fully and independently human. At the same time, each is naturally oriented toward the other, existing in a mutual relationship of belonging.
*James H. Olthuis, I Pledge You My Troth*

The language that God hears best is the silent language of love.
*St. John of the Cross*

To be closer to God, be closer to people.
*Kahlil Gibran*

If thou hast abundance, give alms accordingly: if thou have but a little, be not afraid to give according to that little.
*The Apocrypha, Tobit 4:8*

I always think of nature as a great spectacle, somewhat resembling the opera.
*Bernard de Fontenelle*

Sit down and feed, and welcome to our table.
*William Shakespeare, As You Like It*

Nowhere does the Torah say, Invite your guest to pray; but it does tell us to offer him food, drink and a bed.
*Kagan*

That which doesn't sprout into grass, doesn't sprout into an ear.
*Old French Proverb, before 15th Century*

Fish, if they tarry on dry land, die: even so monks that tarry outside their cell or abide with men of the world fall away from their vow of quiet. As a fish must return to the sea, so must we to our cell: lest it befall that by tarrying without, we forget the watch within.
*St. Anthony the Great, The Father of Monks*

Deep sky is, of all visual impressions, the nearest akin to feeling.
*Samuel Taylor Coleridge*

Whate'er we leave to God, God does and blesses us.
*Henry David Thoreau*

# Codfish Cakes

| | |
|---|---|
| 4 cups flaked codfish | 2 eggs, well beaten |
| 7 or 8 medium potatoes | 1 grated onion (not too small) |
| ½ to ¾ cup scalded milk | |

Cover fish with cold water and bring to a boil; drain. Cook potatoes and mash. Add scalded milk and beat well. Add eggs and onion and continue beating until mixture is creamy. Stir in flaked fish until well mixed. Form into balls, press flat, and fry lightly on each side.
Makes about 16 to 20 cakes.

Most works are most beautiful without ornament.
*Walt Whitman*

I hate people who are not serious about meals.
*Oscar Wilde, Importance of Being Earnest*

We all find time to do what we really want to do.
*William Feather*

A tree growing out of the ground is as wonderful today as it ever was. It does not need to adopt new and startling methods.
*Robert Henri*

It is not that Christianity has not been tried. It has been tried and found difficult.
*Lord Chesterfield*

I do not know wherein I could be better than the worm. For see: he does the will of his Maker and destroys nothing.
*Hasidic Saying*

The more abundantly water gushes from its source, the less is the source esteemed.
*Russian Proverb*

In empty barns when the harvests fail
You may find some forgotten grain.
*S. J. Imber, When Harvests Fail*

What am I? I am myself a word spoken by God. Can God speak a word that does not have any meaning?
*Thomas Merton*

One should not light a fire unless one wants to cook.
*Danish Proverb*

Each bird and stone, each roof
  and well,
feels the gold foot of autumn
  pass;
each spider binds with glittering
  snare
the splintered bones of grass.
*Laurie Lee*

The world is God's language to
us.
*Simone Weil*

Thought is invisible nature, nature is visible thought.
*Heinrich Heine*

Many meats be loathed naturally,
of some persons, yet we never
saw, read, nor heard of any man

# Tuna Loaf

| | |
|---|---|
| 5 cups soft bread crumbs (about 10 slices bread) | 2 teaspoons salt pepper |
| 3 cups scalded milk | 1 grated onion |
| 7 tablespoons melted butter | ¼ cup chopped celery |
| 3 6½-oz. cans flaked tuna | 1 teaspoon chopped parsley |
| | 7 eggs, separated |

Soak crumbs in scalded milk. Add butter, tuna, seasonings. Beat egg yolks well and add, making sure the
mixture has cooled down first. Beat whites until dry
and fold in lightly. Pour into well-greased baking dish.
Bake at 350° for about 45 minutes, until nicely brown.
Salmon may be substituted for tuna.
  Serves 8.

that naturally hated Bread . . .
because it is the staff of Life.
*Moffett, Health's Improvement, 1655*

Nobody, my darling,
Could call me
A fussy man—
BUT
I do like a little bit of butter to
my bread!
*A. A. Milne, When We Were Very
Young. The King's Breakfast*

This Sacramental Bread, and this
alone, Is that supporting Staff of
Life, with which The stout-faith-
ful Generation Their Gallant

journey take to heav'n.
*J. Beaumont*

Eat bread at pleasure, drink
wine by measure.
*English Proverb, 16th Century*

Moderation is the silken string
running through the pearl chain
of all virtues.
*Joseph Hall, Bishop of Norwich,
1574–1656, Christian Moderation*

That woman came from man's
rib simply and beautifully de-
clares that man and woman together constitute humanity. They
came to each other from each
other; they belong together. Man
cannot understand himself in
relationship to God without expressing simultaneously his relationship to his neighbors, men
and women who along with himself are *adam* (man).
*James H. Olthius, I Pledge You My
Troth*

Put you in this pickle.
*Cervantes, Don Quixote*

Union gives strength.
*Aesop, The Bundle of Sticks*

Give ear, my children, to my
  words,
Whom God hath dearly bought,
Lay up his laws within your heart
And print them in your thought.
*John Rogers, Advice to His
Children, a few days before his
martyrdom. (From The New England
Primer)*

We carry with us the wonders we
seek without us.
*Sir Thomas Browne*

Thy sacred emblems to partake
Thy consecrated bread to take
And thine immortal wine!
*Emily Dickinson*

Who riseth from a feast with that keen appetite that he sits down?
*William Shakespeare, Merchant of Venice*

# Eggplant Omelet

½ eggplant (or 1 if small) cut in thin slices or pieces a little bigger than French fried potatoes
2 cloves garlic, minced

1 large onion
4 eggs
1 teaspoon cornstarch
1 cup milk
¼ teaspoon salt
pinch pepper

Fry eggplant, garlic, and onions gently in a little oil or margarine until done (about 5–10 minutes). Beat the eggs. Make paste of cornstarch with a little milk, add remaining milk, and mix well with eggs and seasoning. Pour mixture over the cooked eggplant and cook as an omelet.
 Serves 4.

The trees that grow on the mountain
All go their separate ways.
Some are born to be carved into saints,
Some as charcoal end their days.
*Spanish Rhyme*

The secret of fine painting is to render the invisible.
*Eugène Fromentin*

Our judgement ripens; our imagination decays. We cannot at once enjoy the flowers of the Spring of life and the fruits of its Autumn.
*Thomas Macaulay*

May those who sow in tears reap with shouts of joy!
*Psalm 126:5, RSV*

The stomach is the teacher of the arts and the dispenser of invention.
*Persius, Satires*

Filberts, cob nuts and walnuts should be preserved in sand and salt to prevent them from drying up and decaying.
*Mrs. Beeton's Household Management*

If we deliberately cause suffering and disease in other lives, we increase our own suffering and disease.
*Alicia McInnes*

There is not stopping place in this life—no, nor is there ever one for any man, no matter how far along his way he's gone.
*Meister Eckhart*

Adopt the pace of nature: her secret is patience.
*Ralph Waldo Emerson*

Whoever strives to withdraw from obedience, withdraws from grace.
*Thomas a Kempis*

Sauces are to cookery what grammar is to language and melody is to music.
*Careme and Soyer, Master Chefs*

Music is the sound of universal laws promulgated.
*Henry David Thoreau*

All singers have this fault, that they never can be found ready to sing, when they are asked to perform among friends.
*Horace*

There is no more lovely, friendly and charming relationship, communion or company than a good marriage.
*Martin Luther*

Speaking personally, I have found the happiness of parenthood greater than any other that I have experienced.
*Bertrand Russell*

# Roman Gnocchi

*(Gnocchis à la romaine)*

| | |
|---|---|
| 2 cups milk | 2 tablespoons butter |
| dash nutmeg, salt | 1 cup grated cheese, |
| ¾ cup farina | Italian preferred |
| 2 eggs plus 1 yolk, beaten slightly | |

Scald milk with nutmeg and salt. When just at boiling point, sprinkle in farina while stirring. Keep stirring as farina thickens. Turn off heat and stir in eggs, then ½ the cheese. Pour into an 8–inch square pan and smooth surface so thickness is even. Chill thoroughly. Cut the cold gnocchi into squares, diamond-shapes, etc. Place the pieces on an ovenproof, buttered platter. Dot butter on top; sprinkle with remainder of cheese. Bake for 10 minutes in *preheated* 425° oven.

Serves 4.

We cannot fail in following nature.
*Montaigne*

Love does no wrong to a neighbor; therefore love is the fulfilling of the law.
*Romans 13:10* RSV

Like the best wine . . . that goeth down sweetly, causing the lips of those that are asleep to speak.
*Song of Solomon 7:9,* RSV

To invite people to dine with us is to make ourselves responsible for their well-being for as long as they are under our roofs.
*Anthelme Brillat-Savarin*

Now, good digestion wait on appetite, and health on both!
*William Shakespeare, Macbeth*

God Himself is the best Poet, And the Real is his song.
*Elizabeth Barrett Browning*

He who chews well will feel it in his heels.
*German Proverb*

A man's being in a good and bad humor depends upon his will.
*Samuel Johnson*

God is always opening His hand.
*Spanish Proverb*

Sit down and feed, and welcome to our table.
*William Shakespeare, Merchant of Venice*

What a world of gammon and spinach it is though, ain't it!
*Charles Dickens*

Life must be understood backwards. But . . . it must be lived forwards.
*Sören Kierkegaard*

Out of the kitchen comes the tune.
*Irish Proverb*

The fruit of the papyrus does not surpass an ear of corn.
*Irish Proverb*

There is no love sincerer than the love of food.
*George Bernard Shaw*

During the reign of Louis XIV, writers were drunkards; they but followed the fashion, and the memoirs of that period are very edifying on the subject. Today writers are gourmands, which is a great improvement.
*Anthelme Brillat-Savarin*

Unquiet meals make ill digestions.
*William Shakespeare, A Comedy of Errors*

Take thy thoughts to bed with thee, for the morning is wiser than the evening.
*Russian Proverb*

# Quiche Lorraine

*9″ pie shell:*

| | |
|---|---|
| 1½ cups flour | 6 tablespoons butter |
| ¼ teaspoon salt | ¼ cup water |
| 3 tablespoons margarine | (approximately) |

Work flour, salt, and shortenings; sprinkle on water until dough will just hold in ball but is not sticky. Refrigerate dough (covered) at least 2 hours, preferably more. Roll out and partially bake for 5 to 10 minutes at 375°. Cool.

*Filling:*

| | |
|---|---|
| ¼ lb. bacon (optional) | pinch of nutmeg |
| ½ cup grated Swiss cheese | salt, pepper |
| 3 eggs | 2 tablespoons butter |
| 2 cups milk (or 1 cup milk and 1 cup cream) | |

Fry and drain the bacon. Place it on the pie shell. (Also the cheese, if desired). Beat eggs and milk together; season. Pour mixture into pastry shell. Dot butter on top. Bake in preheated oven at 375° for 30 minutes or until browned on top.
Serves 6.

The sun will set without thy assistance.
*Talmud*

The best thing against worry is to take care of others right away.
*Carl Hilty*

The corn that makes the holy
bread
By which the soul of man is fed,
The holy bread, the food
unpriced,
Thy everlasting mercy, Christ.
*John Masefield*

The Sweeping up the Heart,
And putting Love away
We shall not want to use again
Until Eternity.
*Emily Dickinson*

The truth is found when men are free to pursue it.
*Franklin D. Roosevelt*

So oft goeth the pitcher to the well, that at last it commeth broken home.
*Withals, 1616*

The very first step towards success in any occupation is to become interested in it.
*Sir William Osler*

Let broth boil slowly, but let porridge make a noise.
*Irish Proverb*

Let the songs be loud and cheerful, and not chirpings or pulings.
*Francis Bacon*

Sometimes it happens that love is sweetly awakened in the soul and joyfully arises and stirs itself in the heart without any help

## Oatmeal Pancakes

(*Galettes de flocons d'avoine*)

| | |
|---|---|
| 1⅓ cups water, with pinch salt | 1 medium onion, chopped fine |
| 1⅓ cups oatmeal | butter or oil for frying |
| ¾ cup grated Swiss cheese | parsley, chopped |
| 2 eggs, beaten | |

Bring water to boil; stir in oatmeal and cook 3 to 5 minutes, until consistency is very firm. Add cheese, beaten eggs, onion. Mix thoroughly. (The dough must be quite stiff. It is good, though not necessary, to make it in advance and let it chill.) Heat oil or butter in frying pan or griddle. Spoon oatmeal mixture onto hot pan, brown pancakes on both sides, then reduce heat and cook a total of 20 minutes. Garnish with parsley.

Makes about 8 4-inch pancakes.

from human acts.
*Beatrice of Nazareth, 12th century Beguine*

There is an hour wherein a man might be happy all his life, could he find it.
*George Herbert*

God is more glorified by a man who used the good things of this life in simplicity and with gratitude than by the nervous asceticism of someone who is agitated about every detail of his self-denial . . . His [the latter's] struggle for perfection becomes a kind of battle of wits with the Creator

who made all things good.
*Thomas Merton*

To plow is to pray—to plant is to prophesy, and the harvest answers and fulfills.
*R. G. Ingersoll, About Farming in Illinois*

Where the roads dip and where the roads rise
Seek only there
Where the grey light meets the green air
The hermit's chapel, the pilgrim's prayer.
*T. S. Eliot, Landscapes*

The basest thing in man is his thirst for fame, but that in itself is the clearest sign of his excellence because, whatever possessions he may have on earth, however good his health and however well provided he may be with essentials, he remains unsatisfied unless he enjoys people's good opinion. He sets such high store on reason that, whatever his worldly advantages, unless he is well endowed with it, he is not satisfied. He may have the best place in the world, but nothing can deflect him from this wish, and that is the most indelible quality in the heart of man.

And those who most despise men and put them on the same level as the animals, nevertheless wish to be admired and believed by them, and then contradict themselves by their own feeling; their nature, which is stronger than anything, is more effective in convincing them of man's greatness than reason in persuading them of their baseness.
*Pascal*

Daughters, don't let's give way to disappointment when through obedience we are occupied with external things. If your job is in the kitchen, don't forget that Our Lord is there in the midst of the pots and pans!
*St. Teresa of Avila, Foundations*

What is he better for his wish, when it rains porridge to want a dish.
*Poor Robin's Almanac*

The picture of the mind revives
again:
While here I stand, not only with
the sense
Of present pleasure, but with
pleasing thoughts
That in this moment there is life
and food
For future years.
*William Wordsworth*

The less you eat, the less you ail.
*Zabara, Sefer Shaashuim*

There is a universal law . . .
which none can amend or repeal,
and against which no protest or
preachment can avail, a law . . .
most persistent and inexorable,
the law of eating.
*Mendelé*

I am convinced that the truest
act of courage, the strongest act
of manliness is to sacrifice ourselves for others in a totally non-
violent struggle for justice. To
be a man is to suffer for others.
God help us to be men!
*Cesar Chavez*

And you may see that now the
soul is like a housewife who has
put all her household in good
order.
*Beatrice of Nazareth, 12th century
Beguine*

# Rice Pudding

(*Riz aux oeufs*)

| | |
|---|---|
| 1 cup rice | pinch of nutmeg |
| 1 cup *boiling* water | ½ to 1 cup raisins |
| 3 cups milk | (optional) |
| 3 eggs | 1 teaspoon cinnamon |
| ½ cup sugar | (optional) |
| 1 teaspoon vanilla | |

Preheat oven to 350°. Combine rice and boiling water.
Cover and let sit 40 minutes or until all water is absorbed. (Rice will be partially cooked.) Beat together
all other ingredients. Butter a deep baking dish; pour
in rice and cover with egg mixture. Bake for 50 minutes
or until custard is firm.
    Serves 8.

For the ear tests words, as the
palate tastes food.
*Job 34:3,* RSV

There, then, is the role of the
amateur: to look the world back
to grace. . . . Indeed, the whole
distinction between art and trash,
between food and garbage, depends on the presence or absence
of the loving eye. Turn a statue
over to a boor, and his boredom
will break it to bits—witness the
ruined monuments of antiquity.
On the other hand, turn a shack
over to a lover; for all its
poverty, its lights and shadows
warm a little, and its numbered

surfaces prickle with feeling.
*Father Capon, The Supper Of The
Lamb*

The world needs men who are
free from its demands, men who
are not alienated by its servitudes

in any way. The monastic vocation is traditionally regarded as
a charism of liberty in which the
monk does not simply turn his
back on the world, but on the
contrary becomes free with the
perfect freedom of the sons of
God.
*Thomas Merton*

Do as your children do. They go
to bed at night and sleep without
worries. They don't care whence
they will get soup or bread
tomorrow; they know that Father
and Mother will take care of it.
*Martin Luther*

No child can be born except
through pleasure and joy. By the
same token, if one wishes his
prayers to bear fruit, he must offer them with pleasure and joy.
*Hasidic Saying*

As we *are* and have the divine
being within, we bless each task
we do, be it eating, or sleeping,
or watching, or any other.
*Meister Eckhart*

There is no duty we so much
underrate as the duty of being
happy.
*Robert Louis Stevenson*

The crop of the fields is always rich in hope.
*Spanish Proverb*

For us the winds do blow,
The earth doth rest, heav'n move, and fountains flow.
Nothing we see but means our good,
As our delight, or as our treasure;
The whole is either our cupboard of food,
Or cabinet of pleasure.
*George Herbert*

Do what is good and seek peace in everything.
*St. John of the Cross*

In addition to sorghum and buckwheat other new crops which were even more important were introduced into the Mediterranean region; rice, sugar cane, cotton and mulberry trees. Either the Greeks in the sixth century or the Arabs in the tenth introduced them. Citrus fruits, lemons and bitter oranges, were brought to the south of the peninsula and tended to spread to the north where sweet oranges and other citrus were found around Lake Garda in the thirteenth century, and rice and even a little sugar cane appeared in the Lombardy plain. New varieties of vine were developed during the Middle Ages, the *trebbiano* in Tuscany, the *vernaccia* in Liguria and the *schiava* in the Po valley, and con-

# Pumpkin Pearsauce
(*Compote assaisonnée*)

| | |
|---|---|
| 10 medium pears or apples | 2 tablespoons grated orange rind (great with pears; optional with apples) |
| ½ small pumpkin dash nutmeg | |
| ½ cup sugar (vary according to tartness of fruit) | 1 teaspoon cinnamon (optional) |

Wash fruits; it is not necessary to peel them. Cut fruit into chunks and remove seeds. Put into a heavy pot, with the sugar, orange rind, nutmeg and cinnamon (if used). Cover. Cook over low heat for about an hour, stirring occasionally, until fruits are tender. Put through food grinder, ricer, or blender and chill. Serve very cold.
Serves 8.

centration upon wine production was such that Italian wines entered the export trade. In France most of the areas that today make the best wines were developed in the medieval period.
*Gerald A. J. Hodgett, A Social and Economic History of Medieval Europe*

Since our life as monks consists mainly in singing the praise of God, then, everything around us must also sing. Sing with fruitfulness, with the radiance of beauty. Sing the truth . . . in silence.
*A Contemplative Monk*

Though thou shouldst feel naught, pray inwardly. Pray inwardly, though thou feelest naught, though thou seest naught, yea though it seemeth thou canst not pray for dryness and barrenness. In sickness and in feebleness thy prayer is full pleasant to me (though thou seemingly hast but little savour for it), and so is all thy living prayer in my sight.
*Julian of Norwich, 13th century Anchoress*

The best cure for the body is to quiet the mind.
*Napoleon*

Set him before a hedgerow in a lane,
And he was happy all alone for hours.
*Robert Buchanan, Edward Crowhurst*

How humble the tool when praised for what the hand has done.
*Dag Hammarskjöld, Markings*

Some people despise the little things in life. It is their mistake, for they thus prevent themselves from getting God's greatness out of these little things.
*Meister Eckhart*

Hungry tree!
Your knife branches
Cut the pie-moon into tempting
      pieces.
*Nathan Altshuler, age 13, United
States*

Fair fruit in an unwholesome dish
Are like to rot untasted.
*William Shakespeare*

God intended the earth and all
that it contains for the use of
every human being and people.
Thus, as all men follow justice
and unite in charity, created
goods should abound for them
on a reasonable basis. . . . A man
should regard his lawful possessions not merely as his own but
also as common property in the
sense that they should acrue to
the benefit of not only himself
but of others. . . . The right to
have a share of earthly goods

# Pumpkin Pearsauce Pudding

3 eggs
2 cups milk
1 teaspoon vanilla
2 cups pumpkin pear-
  sauce or pumpkin
  applesauce

1 teaspoon cinnamon
  (if not used in sauce)
⅛ teaspoon ground
  ginger
1 tablespoon butter

Preheat oven to 350°. Beat eggs well; add liquids, then
all other ingredients. Place in a 2 quart baking dish
which is set in a pan of hot water. Bake about 1 hour,
until custard sets.
      Serves 6 to 8.

sufficient for oneself and one's
family belongs to everyone. If a
person is in extreme necessity,
he has the right to take from the
riches of others what he himself
needs.
*Vatican Council II, The Church in the
Modern World, The Radical Bible*

Jack Sprat could eat no fat,
His wife could eat no lean;
And so betwixt them both,
They licked the platter clean.
*Mother Goose*

Rather than just eating something
to satisfy the pangs of hunger,
we can become more perceptive

about food. This may have un-
anticipated repercussions, for
such sensitivity means a deepening of our awareness of all that
surrounds us, thus providing
more satisfaction from the environment.
*Alan Hooker, Vegetarian Gourmet
Cookery*

Good painting is like good cooking—it can be tasted, but not ex-
plained.
*Maurice de Vlaminck*

Silence is the essential condition
of happiness.
*Heinrich Heine*

Cooking is the oldest of all arts:
Adam was born hungry, and
every new child, almost before he
is actually in the world, utters
cries which only his wet nurse's
breast can quiet.
*Anthelme Brillat-Savarin*

It is an unfortunate human failing
that a full pocketbook often
groans more loudly than an
empty stomach.
*Franklin D. Roosevelt, Speech,
Brooklyn, November 1, 1940*

The idea that only a limited
number of people can live in a
country is a profound illusion. It
all depends on their cooperative
and inventive power. There is no
limit to the ingenuity of man if it
is properly and vigorously applied
under conditions of peace and
justice.
*Winston Churchill*

For all this, nature is never spent;
There lives the dearest freshness
      deep down things.
*Gerard Manley Hopkins*

We cannot be just if we are not
kind-hearted.
*Vauvenargues*

Praise the Lord for He is good;
He covers the heavens with
clouds;
He prepares the rain for the
earth,
making mountains sprout with
grass
and plants to serve man's needs.
He provides the beasts with their
food
and young ravens that call upon
him.
The Lord delights in those who
revere him
in those who wait for his love.

*Psalm 146:8, 9, 11*

For I have known them all already, known them all—
Have known the evenings, morn-
ings, afternoons,
I have measured out my life
with coffee spoons.

*T. S. Eliot, The Wasteland*

He is not thirsty who doesn't
drink water.

*Old French Proverb, before 15th
Century*

I remember my youth and the
feeling that will never come back

# Quick Mocha Cookies
(*Petits mokas express*)

6 tablespoons butter
1 cup powdered sugar
1 egg yolk
1 heaping teaspoon in-
stant coffee

8 to 12 tea biscuits
(plain, slightly sweet
cookies, English or
Belgian type)

Cream butter, sugar, and egg yolk; when smooth, work
in the coffee. Spread on the cookies. It's nice to make
an attractive design—swirl, for example—with the
back of the spoon.

any more—the feeling that I
could last forever, outlast the sea,
the earth, and all men.

*Joseph Conrad*

Holy God, Holy Mighty One,
Holy Immortal One. Have mercy
on us (3 times).

*Ancient Christian Prayer*

Not to be able to grow old is just
as ricidulous as to be unable to
outgrow childhood.

*C. G. Jung*

Acquire the art of detachment,
the virtue of method, and the

quality of thoroughness, but
above all the grace of humility.

*Sir William Osler*

To know how to grow old is the
master work of wisdom, and one

of the most difficult chapters in
the great art of living.

*Frédéric Amiel*

'Tis solitude should teach us how
to die;
It hath no flatterers; vanity can
give
No hollow aid; alone—man with
his God must strive.

*Lord Byron, Childe Harold's
Pilgrimage*

O God, Our Father, we come to
You at the close of day, for You
are the light that never fades.

*Roman Breviary*

Beautiful are the skies, the sun,
the moon and the stars, and all
things made by God, but man is
the most beautiful of all; for he
bears within himself a beauty
created to the image of God!

*St. Tychon*

'Tis one of the great gifts of mind
to be able to offer what is needed
at the moment.

*Baltasar Gracián*

# Quick Apple Cake
(*Gâteau aux pommes*)

| | |
|---|---|
| 2 eggs | ⅓ cup oil |
| ⅓ cup milk | 4 apples, peeled, cored, cut in thick (¼-inch) slices |
| 2 teaspoons baking powder | |
| 6 tablespoons sugar or light brown sugar | ½ cup cream or condensed milk |
| ¾ cup whole wheat flour | 1 teaspoon cinnamon |
| small pinch salt | |

Preheat oven to 350°. Butter an 8-inch baking pan. Beat eggs well; add milk. Combine dry ingredients (*not* cinnamon) and beat into egg mixture; beat in oil. Dough is quite firm and thick. Spread dough in pan. Stand the apple slices on edge over entire surface of dough. Bake 15 minutes. Remove from oven, pour cream over surface and sprinkle with cinnamon; return to oven for another 25 minutes.

My soul into the boughs does glide:
There like a bird it sits, and sighs,
Then whets and combs its longer flight,
Waves in its plumes the various light.
*Andrew Marvell, The Garden*

Such as is the tree, such fruits thereof wee see.
*English Proverb, 16th Century*

Manners are of more importance than laws.
*Edmund Burke*

Good manners is the art of making those people easy with whom we converse. Whoever makes the fewest persons uneasy is the best bred in the company.
*Jonathan Swift*

An apple a day keeps the doctor away.
*Anonymous*

It is better to know some of the questions than all of the answers.
*James Thurber*

A good question is never answered. It is not a bolt to be tightened into place but a seed to be planted and to bear more seed toward the hope of greening the landscape of idea. The difference between a seed and an inert speck can be hard to see, but only one of them will grow and return itself in kind and be multiplied.
*John Ciardi*

A visitor strolling through the noble woods of Ferney complimented Voltaire on the splendid growth of his trees. "Ay," he replied, "they have nothing else to do," and walked on without another word. The tree which moves some to tears of joy is in the eyes of others only a green thing that stands in the way.
*William Blake*

The greatest masterpieces were once only pigments on a palette.
*Henry S. Haskins*

What wondrous life is this I lead!
Ripe apples drop about my head;
The luscious clusters of the vine
Upon my mouth do crush their wine;
The nectarine, and curious peach,
Into my hands themselves do reach;
Stumbling on melons, as I pass,
Ensnared with flowers, I fall on grass.
Here at the fountain's sliding foot
Or at some fruit-tree's mossy root,
Casting the body's vest aside,

Simplicity reaches out after God, purity discovers and enjoys Him.
*Thomas a Kempis*

I think today the world is upside-down, and is suffering so much because there is so very little love in the homes, and in family life. We have no time for our children, we have no time for each other; there is no time to enjoy each other, and I think if we could only bring back into our lives the life that Jesus, Mary and Joseph lived in Nazareth, if we could make our homes another Nazareth, I think that peace and joy would reign in the world.
*Mother Teresa of Calcutta*

The Pedigree of Honey
Does not concern the Bee
A Clover, any time, to him,
Is aristocracy.
*Emily Dickinson*

I will arise and go now, and go
  to Innisfree,
And a small cabin build there, of
  clay and wattles made;
Nine bean-rows will I have there,
  a hive for the honeybee,
And live alone in the bee-loud
  glade.
And I shall have some peace
  there, for peace comes
  dropping slow.
*William Butler Yeats*

The soul that projects itself
entirely into activity, and seeks
itself outside itself in the work of
its own will is like a madman
who sleeps on the sidewalk in
front of his house instead of living
inside where it is quiet and warm.
*Thomas Merton*

# Honey Applesauce Cake

⅓  cup shortening
¾  cup honey
1  cup hot unsweetened
   applesauce
1  to 1½ cups sifted flour
¼  teaspoon each cloves,
   ginger, and
   cinnamon

1  cup chopped seedless
   raisins
½  cup chopped nuts (if
   desired)
2  teaspoons baking soda
1  tablespoon hot water

Cream shortening and honey. Add warm applesauce. Sift together flour and spices and sprinkle over the raisins and nuts. Next mix together all the ingredients except the soda. Dissolve soda in hot water and mix it in last. Bake in greased, floured loaf pan at 325° for about 1 hour.

The key to the world is humility. Without it all hustling, listening, watching is in vain.
*Christian Morgenstern*

The pride in the cup is in the drink, its humility in the serving. What, then, do its defects matter?
*Dag Hammarskjöld, Markings*

Let me say, at the risk of seeming ridiculous, that the true revolutionary is guided by great feelings of love.
*Che Guevara*

As thou yieldest no honey,

wound not with thy sting.
*Persian Proverb*

Fair love, let us go play:
Apples ben ripe in my gardayne.
I shall thee clothe in new array,
Thy meat shall be milk, honey
  and wine.
Fair love, let us go dine:
Thy sustenance is in my crippe,
  lo!
Tarry thou not, my fair spouse
  mine.
*Anonymous*

If my tongue is covered with a bitter coating, then however

sweet the wine, it will taste bitter, because of the coating through which it reaches me. This is how it is with the person who, having given up all that is his own, is coated with God, so that no creature can touch him without first touching God, and whatever reaches him must reach him through God.
*Meister Eckhart*

The most beautiful of all emblems is that of God, whom Timaeus of Locris describes under the image of "A circle whose center is everywhere and circumference nowhere."
*Voltaire*

The first unit of society is the family. The family should look after its own and, in addition, as the early Fathers said, "Every home should have a Christ room in it, so that hospitality may be practiced."
*Dorothy Day*

My son, eat honey, for it is good, and the drippings of the honeycomb are sweet to your taste.
*Proverbs 24:13, RSV*

I did not know the ample bread;
'Twas so unlike the crumb
The birds and I had often shared.
*Emily Dickinson*

All nature is meant to make us think of paradise. Woods, fields, valleys, hills, the rivers and the sea, the clouds traveling across the sky, light and darkness, sun and stars, remind us that the world was first created as a paradise for the first Adam.
*Thomas Merton*

First there is needed a clerk or varlet, to purchase greenery, violets, chaplets, milk, cheese, eggs, logs, coal, salt, vats and washing tubs both for the dining hall and for the butteries, verjuice, vinegar, sorrel, sage, parsley, fresh garlic, two brooms, a shovel and other small things.
*G. G. Coulton and Eileen Power, eds. The Goodman of Paris (Le Ménagier de Paris)*

And he told them a parable, saying, "The land of a rich man brought forth plentifully; and he thought to himself, 'What shall I do, for I have nowhere to store my crops?' And he said, 'I will

# Spoon Bread

| | | | |
|---|---|---|---|
| 1 | cup yellow corn meal | 4 | beaten egg yolks |
| 1⅓ | cups cold milk | 2 | teaspoons baking powder |
| 2 | cups scalded milk | | |
| 2 | tablespoons butter | 4 | stiffly beaten egg whites |
| 1½ | teaspoons salt | | |

Mix corn meal with the cold milk. Slowly stir into scalded milk and cook until mixture thickens, stirring frequently. Add butter and salt. Cool this mixture and then add egg yolks and baking powder. Fold in stiffly beaten egg whites and pour mixture into greased 2-quart soufflé or casserole dish. Bake at 350° about 50 minutes or until puffed and brown.

do this: I will pull down my barns, and build larger ones; and

there I will store all my grain and my goods. And I will say to my soul, Soul, you have ample goods laid up for many years; take your ease, eat, drink, be merry.' But God said to him, 'Fool! This night your soul is required of you; and the things you have prepared, whose will they be?' . . . "
*Luke 12:16–20* RSV

Let us seek bread with the plough.
*Juvenal*

Nature is visible thought.
*Heinrich Heine*

O Lord, it is you who are my portion and cup;
it is you yourself who are my prize.
The lot marked out for me is my delight:
welcome indeed the heritage that falls to me!
*Psalm 15:5, 6*

Pursue, keep up with, circle round and round your life, as a dog does his master's chaise. Do what you love. Know your own bone; gnaw at it, bury it, unearth it, and gnaw it still.
*Henry David Thoreau*

The young man who has not wept is a savage, and the old man who will not laugh is a fool.
*George Santayana*

He had a broad face and a little round belly,
That shook, when he laughed, like a bowlful of jelly.
*Clement Clarke Moore, A Visit from St. Nicholas*

To laugh is proper to man.
*François Rabelais*

In almost any region of France the more intricate cooking, the special dish, is saved for the special day: Sunday, of course, but usually a special Sunday, like Easter; or a baptism, a wedding, a betrothal (not necessarily in that order!); above all for birthdays and private family anniversaries like the First Warm Day, The First Frost, The Day in Honor of the Biggest Trout (caught in 1903 by Uncle René), The Last Strawberry Tart until Next Year. These almost childlike excuses to gather together around a dining table are a part of country living that city people try to cling to, with some desperation, amid the increasing pressures of urbanization everywhere, but the French are especially stubborn and even in Paris such festivities are still taken seriously.

*M. F. K. Fisher, The Cooking of Provincial France*

Preach not to others what they should eat, but eat as becomes

# Tart Shell

| | |
|---|---|
| 2 cups flour | ⅜ to ½ lb. butter, margarine, or lard (or ½ of one, ½ of another) |
| 1 teaspoon salt | |
| 1 egg | |
| ½ cup cold water (add a little more if this does not moisten enough) | |

*Basque Tart Shell.* Place the flour with salt added in a mound on table. Make a hole in the center and add the egg which has been beaten in the water until the liquid is completely homogenous. Mix the flour and the egg-water liquid well. Gradually add some butter, in small lumps, throughout the dough. Roll it out, fold over with the palms of the hands. Roll it out, fold it (like a handkerchief), and put it aside for 10 minutes. Repeat 2 more times using the rest of the butter with 10 minute "rests" between each rolling out. Finally roll out and line an 8″ or 9″ pie plate. If there is extra dough, it can be kept for a week or more in the refrigerator.

| | |
|---|---|
| 1½ cups flour | ½ cup water |
| 1¼ teaspoon salt | (approximately) |
| 6 tablespoons butter | |
| 3 tablespoons margarine | |

*French Tart Shell.* Work flour, salt, and shortenings; sprinkle on water until dough will just hold in ball but is not sticky. Refrigerate dough (covered) at least 2 hours, preferably more. Roll out and line a 9″ pie plate.

Both tarts serve 6.

you, and be silent.
*Epictetus*

It is nearly fifty years since I was assured by a conclave of doctors that if I did not eat meat I should die of starvation.
*George Bernard Shaw*

It requires grace to turn a man into a saint, and anyone who doubts it does not know what a saint or what a man is.
*Pascal*

My Aunt Maria asked me to read the life of Dr. Chalmers, which, however, I did not promise to do. Yesterday, Sunday, she was heard through the partition shouting to my Aunt Jane, who is deaf. "Think of it! He stood half an hour today to hear the frogs croak, and he wouldn't read the life of Chalmers."
*Henry David Thoreau*

To make a prairie it takes a clover
and one bee,
One clover, and a bee,
And revery.
The revery alone will do,
If bees are few.
*Emily Dickinson*

To drink pure water go to the source.
*Maltese Proverb*

The eye is bigger than the belly.
*George Herbert*

If I were given my choice between an egg and ambrosia for breakfast, I should choose an egg.
*Robert Lynd*

One egg is as nothing, two doe much good, three is enough, four are too many, five bring death.
*French Proverb*

In general, mankind, since the improvement of cookery, eat twice as much as nature requires.
*Benjamin Franklin*

If specific exercises in self-denial are undertaken, they should be inconspicuous, non-competitive and uninjurious to health. Thus,

---

# Basic Quiche Filling

2 tablespoons flour
1 cup of milk
2 eggs
1 teaspoon vanilla

pinch of salt
raisins (any quantity desired)
4 oz. cheese

Mix the flour with the milk by diluting first with a little milk, then gradually adding the rest so that there are no lumps. Beat the eggs. Combine liquid and eggs, beating together until well mixed. Add seasonings. Pour this into the tart shell. Sprinkle raisins and then the cheese which has been cut into small pieces. Bake at 350°–375° about 30 minutes or until done.
Serves 6.

---

in the matter of diet, most people will find it sufficiently mortifying to refrain from eating all the things which the experts in nutrition condemn as unwholesome.
*Aldous Huxley*

It was as though we expected that land to be hospitable. The fact that it was hospitable, to a degree, was sheer accident. And yet, all through history man has been saying, "I shall live here," and finding the means to live where he chose. Either this earth is a remarkably habitable place or man is a favored creature. I would rather believe in the habit-

ability of the earth, because when man comes to believe too much in his own favor he achieves an unhappy arrogance. The earth has its own pulse and rhythms, and the wise and fortunate man leans with the wind, sows with the season, and searches for water in valleys where water flows.
*Hal Borland*

A cow when it is full walks away from the feeding trough and lies down. The glutton having filled his gut at the table of his craving does not consent to look at another person who is in need, but

---

with total subjection to his own desire he believes there is no one in so great need as he is himself.
*Philoxenus of Mabbog, A.D. 523*

Overindulgence must be avoided and a monk must never be overtaken by indigestion.
*Rule of St. Benedict*

If we leave the jungle and look elsewhere in the animal kingdom for strength, it's interesting to note that only vegetarian animals are used as beasts of burden—the ox, the horse and the mule. And to show you what Mother Nature's soil thinks of the meat-eating habit, only the manure of vegan animals and humans is suitable for fertilizing the growth, life and power of orchard and garden plants!
*Dick Gregory, Dick Gregory's Natural Diet for Folks Who Eat: Cookin' with Mother Nature*

The fullest possible enjoyment is to be found by reducing our ego to zero.
*G. K. Chesterton*

Sermons on diet ought to be preached in the churches at least once a week.
*G. C. Lichtenberg*

Send me some preserved cheese, that when I like I may have a feast.
*Epicurus*

The Queen of Hearts
She made some tarts,
All on a summer's day;
The Knave of Hearts
He stole the tarts,
And took them clean away.

The King of Hearts
Called for the tarts,
And beat the Knave full sore;
The Knave of Hearts
Brought back the tarts,
And vow'd he'd steal no more.
*Anonymous, Nursery Rhymes*

# Cheese Tart Filling

4 oz. any cheese, cut into      seasonings as desired
small bits
mushrooms *or* raisins
(quantity desired)

This tart can be as varied as the seasonings and the cheese you use. Two examples: (1) gruyere and mushrooms, seasoned with salt, pepper, parsley, and nutmeg; or (2) cheddar and raisins and a sprinkle of nutmeg.

Add ingredients to the basic quiche mixture. Pour into the tart shell and bake as for quiche.

# Seafood Tart Filling

clams and shrimp (or any      pinch of salt and pepper
other available seafood)      thyme (to taste)
chopped parsley

Mix well and pour into the tart shell. Bake as for quiche.

Is not this the fast that I choose: to loose the bonds of wickedness, to undo the thongs of the yoke, and to break every yoke? Is it not to share your bread with the hungry, and bring the homeless poor into your house; when you see the naked, to cover him, and not to hide yourself from your own flesh?
*Isaiah 58:6*, RSV

With our bodies we are bound to the earth and food is our umbilical cord. Once it is cut, we are dead. Nothing makes us more aware of our dependence on the earth than when food is scarce.
*Carl and LaVonne Braaten, The Living Temple*

Make your service of love a beautiful thing: want nothing else, fear nothing else and let love be free to become what love truly is.
*Hadewijch of Antwerp, 12th century Beguine*

In holy ways there is never so much must.
*Thomas Merton*

When they had finished breakfast, Jesus said to Simon Peter, "Simon, son of John, do you love me more than these?" He said to him, "Yes, Lord; you know that I love you." He said to him, "Feed my lambs." A second time he said to him, "Simon, son of John, do you love me?" He said to him, "Yes, Lord; you know that I love you." He said to him, "Tend my sheep." He said to him the third time, "Simon, son of John, do you love me?" Peter was grieved because he said to him the third time, "Do you love me?" And he said to him, "Lord, you know everything; you know that I love you." Jesus said to him, "Feed my sheep."
*John 21:15–17*, RSV

It's watering time
In the gardens of Heaven
As raindrops tumble
On cities and towns.
*Richard Drillich, age 9, United States*

From your dwellings You water
    the hills,
earth drinks its fill of your gift.
You make the grass grow for
    the cattle
and the plants to serve man's
    needs,
that they may bring forth bread
    from the earth
and wine to cheer man's heart,
oil, to make his face shine
and bread to strengthen man's
    heart.
*Psalm 103:13–15*

Good temper is an estate for life.
*William Hazlitt*

From his cradle to his grave a
man never does a single thing
which has any first and foremost
object save one—to secure peace
of mind, spiritual comfort, for
himself.
*Mark Twain*

The monk is by definition a man
who lives in seclusion, in solitude, in silence outside of the
noise and confusion of a busy
worldly existence. He does this
because seclusion provides certain necessary conditions for his
life: an interior freedom, silence,
liberation from trivial concerns
that arise from overstimulation
of the appetites and the imagination.
*Thomas Merton*

Nature is the greatest teacher and
I learn from her best when others
are asleep. In the still dark hours
before sunrise God tells me of
the plans I am to fulfill.
*George Washington Carver*

In those days, when again a great
crowd had gathered, and they

# Basque Salmon Tart Filling

1 17-oz. can of salmon
shredded into bits
raisins (any quantity
desired)

sprinkling of salt and
pepper

Add ingredients to the basic quiche mixture. Pour into
the tart shell and bake at 375° for 45 minutes.
    All serve 6.

had nothing to eat, he called his
disciples to him, and said to them,
"I have compassion on the crowd,
because they have been with me
now three days, and have nothing
to eat; and if I send them away
hungry to their homes, they will
faint on the way; and some of
them have come a long way."
And his disciples answered him,
"How can one feed these men
with bread here in the desert?"
And he asked them, "How many
loaves have you?" They said,
"Seven." And he commanded
the crowd to sit down on the
ground; and he took the seven
loaves, and having given thanks
he broke them and gave them to
his disciples to set before the
people; and they set them before
the crowd. And they had a few
small fish; and having blessed
them, he commanded that these

also should be set before them.
And they ate, and were satisfied;
and they took up the broken
pieces left over, seven baskets
full. And there were about four
thousand people.
*Mark 8:1–9,* RSV

O Christ, our true God, bless
this food and drink which we
receive from You. Bless the food
of our neighbors and give bread,
peace, and joy to all mankind.
Amen.
*Table Prayer from Our Lady of the
Resurrection Monastery*

Therefore I say that we must
learn to look through every gift
and every event to God and
never be content with the thing
itself.
*Meister Eckhart*

He who watches over the fig tree
eats its fruit.
*Spanish Proverb*

What wondrous life is this I lead!
Ripe apples drop about my head;
The luscious clusters of the vine
Upon my mouth do crush their
 wine;
The nectarine, and curious peach,
Into my hands themselves do
 reach;

# Apple Compote

2 cups water
1 to 1½ cups sugar (depending on sweetness of apples)

2 lbs. apples (peeled and cored and cut in halves or quarters depending on size)
2 pieces of lemon peel
5 whole cloves

Heat water and sugar together. When the sugar is completely dissolved, add apples, lemon peel, and cloves. Cook about 20 minutes, over high heat. Serve chilled.
 Serves 6.

# Peach Compote

2 lbs. peaches (ripe)     1¼ cups sugar
¾ cup of water

Peel peaches, remove pits, and cut in half. Heat water and sugar together. When sugar is completely dissolved, add peaches. Cook gently over low heat. If the peaches are tender, they should cook in about 15 minutes. You can add 1 tablespoon white wine to enhance taste. (For special delicacy, add 1 tablespoon of your favorite liqueur.)
 Serves 6.

Stumbling on melons, as I pass,
Ensnared with flowers, I fall on
 grass.
Here at the fountain's sliding foot
Or at some fruit-tree's mossy
 root,
Casting the body's vest aside,
My soul into the boughs does
 glide:
There like a bird it sits, and sighs,
Then whets and combs its silver
 wings;
And, till prepared for longer
 flight,
Waves in its plumes the various
 light.
*Andrew Marvell, The Garden*

A tree often transplanted bears
not much fruit.
*English Proverb*

Wormes do eate the fruitfullest
trees.
*English Proverb, 16th Century*

Of what consequence, though our
planet explode, if there is no character involved in the explosion?
In health we have not the least
curiosity about such events. We
do not live for idle amusement. I
would not run round a corner to
see the world blow up.
*Henry David Thoreau*

There is no tree but bears some
fruit.
*English Proverb*

Sugar in the gourd and honey in
 the horn,
I never was so happy since the
 hour I was born.
*Mother Goose*

And God said, "Behold, I have
given you every plant yielding
seed which is upon the face of all
the earth, and with every tree
with seed in its fruit; and you
shall have them for good."
*Genesis 129–30,* RSV

A Garden is a lovesome think
God wot!
*Thomas Edward Brown, My Garden*

The man in the wilderness asked
  me,
How many strawberries grew in
  the sea?
I answered him, as I thought
  good,
As many as red herrings grew in
  the wood.
*Mother Goose*

Inns are the mirror and at the
same time the flower of a people.
*Hilaire Belloc*

All flowers talk to me and so
hundreds of little living things in
the woods. I learn what I know

# Pear Compote

| 2 lbs. pears | ¾ cup water |
| sugar to taste (the | 1¼ cups wine (white |
| original recipe calls | preferred) |
| for 1 lb. sugar!) | |

If the pears are small, peel and leave whole. If they are larger, peel and cut in halves or quarters and remove seeds. Cook together the sugar and liquid, stirring constantly. Remove from the heat as it begins to boil. Add the pears. Cook gently for about 20 minutes. Let cool, and then chill in refrigerator at least 1 hour. Just before serving, add 1 tablespoon rum to the compote.
    Serves 6.

    The apple, pear, and peach compote recipes are somewhat "fancy" dishes. A quicker (and more nutritious) variety, frequently served, is to employ the recipes without peeling the fruit. When the fruit is cooked, put it in a blender. Americans who are more nutrition conscious may prefer to sacrifice finesse and simply employ the compote recipes without peeling the fruit, leaving all the rest as in the recipes. Compotes can be made of mixed fruits, taking care to add those which require longer cooking first.

by watching and loving everything.
*George Washington Carver*

My Lord, Thou art in every
  breath I take,
And every bite and sup taste firm
  of Thee.
*Kenneth E. Boulding, There Is a Spirit*

The first mention of the modern plate in England was in 1641, when they are referred to as 'white earthen trencher plates'. These were five inches across and decorated on one side. You turned this decorated side face down before you helped your-self. At first plates were used not for the main meal, but afterwards in the chamber for eating fruit, creams and comfits that were served when people had risen from the table and withdrawn to what we would call the drawing-room.
*Katie Stewart, Cooking and Eating*

I never found the companion that was so companionable as solitude. We are for the most part more lonely when we go abroad among men than when we stay in our chambers. A man thinking or working is always alone, let him be where he will.
*Henry David Thoreau, Walden*

More exquisite than any other
is the autumn rose.
*Theodore Agrippa D'Aubigné, Les
Tragiques. Les Feux*

Cloyed with ragouts you scorn my
   simple food,
And think good eating is man's
   only good;
I ask no more than temperance
   can give;
You live to eat, I only eat to live.

*Richard Graves, Diogenes to
Aristippus*

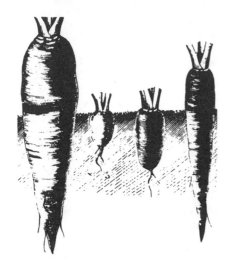

To coin a phrase, mint has more
uses than money. It is excellent
with vegetables, such as carrots
and peas, it cools the palate
when blended with yoghurt and
it adds an interesting touch to
mixed green salads.

*Craig Claiborne, An Herb And Spice
Cook Book*

A good meal ought to begin with
hunger.

*French Proverb*

Root vegetables, protected by
the soil from the worst ravages
of the weather, must always have
been important. Turnips, onions,
and a large type of radish almost
certainly date back to prehistoric times in Europe. Within the
period of recorded history, the
roots of the lotus, asphodel, and
Solomon's-seal, and the rhizomes
of canna lily, have all been eaten

# Savory Carrots

| | |
|---|---|
| 8   medium sized carrots | 1   tablespoon chopped |
| 3   tablespoons butter |      parsley |
| ⅛   teaspoon mustard |      pinch tarragon |
|     powder |      salt and pepper |

Peel, slice, boil carrots. Melt butter. Mix with mois-
tened mustard powder (or prepared mustard). Stir in
carrots, chopped parsley, tarragon, salt and pepper to
taste.
    Serves 6.

# Savory Acorn Squash

| | |
|---|---|
| 3   acorn squash | honey |
|     melted butter | salt, pepper |

Quarter the squash and remove seeds. Place open side
down in pan containing ½ inch water. Bake at 350°
for 30 to 35 minutes. Remove squash from oven and
from pan and paint (baste) with butter and honey.
Sprinkle with salt and pepper.
    Serves 6.

with evident relish, and there
is no reason why such flower
bulbs should not also have
played a part in the diet of
prehistoric man.

*Reay Tannahill, Food In History*

Cooking is also of all the arts the
one which has done most to advance our civilization, for the
needs of the kitchen were what
first taught us to use fire, and it
is by fire that man has tamed Nature itself.

*Anthelme Brillat-Savarin*

It is amazing how many vegetables can be cooked with little
or no added water at all. Even
the hardest ones—like carrots
and turnips—if sliced thin enough
will be twice as flavorful for having been gently wilted rather than
boiled to death. The rule for de-
ciding how much water to use is
simple: Generally speaking, any
cooking water you throw away
is excess water; if you use that
much less, your food will have
that much more taste.

*Father Capon, The Supper of The
Lamb*

Happiness, it seems to me, consists of two things: first, in being
where you belong, and second—
and best—in comfortably going
through everyday life, that is,
having had a good night's sleep
and not being hurt by new shoes.

*Theodor Fontane*

Three things revolutionized table manners and eating habits during the seventeenth century: the fork, the plate and the potato.
*Katie Stewart, Cooking and Eating*

Any old woman can love God better than a doctor of theology can.
*St. Bonaventura*

These are the days when skies put on
The old, old sophistries of June,
A blue and gold mistake.
*Emily Dickinson*

The power to guess the unseen from the seen, to trace the implications of things, to judge the whole piece by the pattern,

# Savory Roast Potatoes

Provide 1 whole potato per person.

Cut potatoes in half. Drop into boiling salted water. Drain well when cooked, about 15 to 20 minutes. Rub potatoes with butter. Sprinkle with garlic salt, summer savory, salt, and pepper. Broil until browned slightly.

the condition of feeling life in general so completely that you are well on your way to knowing any particular corner of it—this cluster of gifts may almost be said to constitute experience.
*Henry James, The Art of Fiction*

I had three chairs in my house: one for solitude, two for friendship, three for society.
*Henry David Thoreau, Walden*

Simplification of outward life is not enough. It is merely the outside. But I am starting with the

outside. I am looking at the outside of a shell, the outside of my life—the shell. The complete answer is not to be found on the outside, in an outward mode of living. This is only a technique, a road to grace. The final answer, I know, is always inside. But the outside can give a clue, can help one to find the inside answer. One is free, like the hermit crab, to change one's shell.
*Anne Morrow Lindbergh, Gift from the Sea*

Parsley is most frequently used either chopped or in the leaf as

a garnish for dishes, but it is delicious when used in large quantities as a pronounced seasoning. Like mint, it is one of the

easiest of herbs to grow. Generally, there are two kinds of parsley available, the curly variety and the flat leaf, which is also called Italian parsley. Raw parsley is said to sweeten the breath.
*Craig Claiborne, An Herb And Spice Cook Book*

And for all this, nature is never spent;
There lives the dearest freshness deep down things.
*Gerard Manley Hopkins, God's Grandeur*

Why does a scientist work in a laboratory, or why does a sailor go on a ship or why does a duck swim in water? Why does a man go to his bedroom and get in bed when he wants to sleep? Why doesn't he lie down in the middle of the street? A monk seeks silence and solitude because there his mind and heart can relax and expand and attain to a new perspective.
*Thomas Merton*

A sight of happiness is happiness.
*Thomas Traherne*

Man was sent by God into the world of nature in order to cultivate it and to offer it back to Him.
*Paul Claudel*

The hills are alive with the sound of music,
With songs they have sung for a thousand years.
*Oscar Hammerstein*

By matter we are nourished,

# Fruit Tart Fillings

*Basic cream filling:*

2 tablespoons corn-
  starch dissolved in a
  little milk
2 cups milk
2 eggs

1 teaspoon vanilla (2
  teaspoons if it is arti-
  ficial vanilla)
¼ cup sugar

Dilute the cornstarch in a little of the milk (cold, or just warm). Beat eggs. Combine beaten eggs, vanilla, sugar, and cornstarch mixture and beat briefly to be sure it is well combined.

Bring the milk to a boil. As it comes to a boil, add the other ingredients and stir rapidly. Cook, stirring continually, 2–3 minutes only. Let cool. When the liquid has cooled, pour it into the basic tart shell. Arrange fruit slices on top.

*Apple:* 4 apples, peeled and sliced fine. Arrange in rings on top of the cream.

*Pears, cherries*, or *prunes* can also be used.

*Basque fruit tart:* 2 apples, peeled and sliced fine, 2 bananas sliced, raisins (quantity desired).

Serves 6.

lifted up, linked to everything else, invaded by life.
*Pierre Teilhard de Chardin, The Divine Milieu*

Gather up the fragments left over, that nothing may be lost.
*John 6:12*, RSV

Love, on the contrary, sustains the artist. Love is an important thing, the greatest good, which alone renders light that which weighs heavy, and bears with an equal spirit that which is unequal. For it carries weights which without it would be a burden, and makes sweet and pleasant all that is bitter. . . Love wants to rise, not to be held down by anything base. . . Nothing is more gentle than love, nothing stronger, nothing higher, nothing larger, nothing more pleasant, nothing more complete, nothing better in heaven or on earth—because love is born of God and cannot rest other than in God, above all living beings. He who loves, flies, runs, and rejoices; he is free and nothing holds him back.
*Matisse*

When Earth's last picture is
  painted, and the tubes are
  twisted and dried,
When the oldest colors have
  faded, and the youngest critic
  has died,
We shall rest, and, faith, we
  shall need it—lie down for
  an eon or two,
Till the Master of All Good
  Workmen shall put us to
  work anew.
*Rudyard Kipling*

# Herbal Teas for All Seasons

Americans are just discovering the herb teas used in Europe for millennia. In the United States, however, they are generally expensive since most are imported. Herb teas are simply dried leaves and/or flowers over which boiling water is poured, and the mixture is then steeped several minutes. Some plants are stimulating, and some are calming, more often the latter. For this reason, Europeans usually serve herb teas at the end of a meal (to aid digestion) or in the evening or before retiring.

**General Rule for Herb Teas.** Pour boiling water over a few sprigs of any herb, cover, and let stand 3 to 5 minutes. Generally 2 or 3 sprigs are used for a small pot (2 to 4 servings). Since different plants have different properties, experiment with the proportion of leaf to water and time of steeping to get the flavor and strength you prefer. A few herb teas are better boiled 2 to 3 minutes before steeping, but the above rule is good for any type and is preferable for most. Here are 3 varieties you can make at home.

**Orange Tea.** Save the peels from oranges, peeling them insofar as possible in one long strip. Peel as thinly as possible, trying to peel off the orange and leave the white inner skin. (You will inevitably get a little white, but try to have the least possible.) These orange peels can be kept (at a cool room temperature) until dried out some. Use the peel of 1 orange for 3 to 4 cups of tea, following the above general rule. Let steep 4 to 5 minutes and serve. Sweeten to taste.

**Mint Tea.** Mint is easy to grow in any sunny corner of the garden or indoors. It can be used fresh or dried; the flavors of each are slightly different, so try both. In the case of all *fresh* leaves used to make herb tea, cut up the leaves before pouring on the boiling water since more flavor is released.

**Linden Tea.** If you have space enough to have a linden tree in your yard or nearby, you can have unlimited quantities of one of the best herb teas. (In France linden (*tilleul*) is the most common herb tea (*infusion*). When the linden tree is in flower, pick as many sprigs as you think you will want in a year. Pick 3 or 4 inches at the ends of sprigs where there are flowers in bloom (flowers which are fully open and not faded). Pick just the flower and the narrow light green leaves next to it, not the large leaves of the tree. Dry by laying them out on any surface in a shady place since sunlight spoils the flavor. When thoroughly dried, they can be stored in bottles or plastic bags and used as needed.

# Useful Culinary Instructions

**Steaming** Cooks faster, retains vitamins and minerals. One can steam all vegetables which we usually boil.

**Yogurt** It is worthwhile to buy a yogurt maker, since it pays for itself in several months. If yogurt is made with dry milk, it is very inexpensive. It is also very nutritious.

**Grains and Beans** Each has an incomplete protein. When used in combination, produces a complete protein.

**Tomato Sauce** Always cook some carrot in it, for taste.

**Wheat Germ** Use it often for cheapest high quality nutrition. Use it in broth instead of noodles or rice. Use in matzo balls; as layers in a casserole; as topping instead of bread crumbs; as a thickener.

**Hi-Protein Matzo Balls** Follow recipe on matzo meal box, doubling egg and adding ½ cup wheat germ. Add balls to broth, soup, or stew.

**Whole Grains** Rye, soy, buckwheat, whole wheat. Buy in health food stores. Use in cooking or, for even more nutrition and increased digestibility, sprout: just cover some grains with water. Change water and rinse every 8 hours. Takes 30 to 36 hours to sprout. Grains are crunchy and nutritious.

**Brown Rice** For greater nutrition never use white rice. Substitute brown.

**Oils** Use only cold pressed. Vitamins D and E are normally eliminated in usual commercial hot pressing. Try to vary the oils you use in salads and cooking for more of a spectrum of vitamins and minerals: safflower, soy, walnut, peanut, corn.

**"Pseudosautéing technique": delicious and healthy** To give a sautéed taste without indigestibility of fried foods: instead of sautéing in butter or oils, cook in just enough slightly sugared water or broth so that when fully cooked water is all absorbed and food is beginning to stick to the pan and burn a little. Quickly pour in a little cold-pressed oil; stir it up well and scrape all the brown which had begun to burn. (This retains all the vitamins from vegetables and oil, uses oil as seasoning, and still gives the sautéed taste. Recommended for carrots, greens, potatoes, parsnips, onions, string beans, broccoli, etc.) People who can't digest fried foods can eat these. Salt and pepper to taste after cooking.

**Curry** Is very digestible. (OK for persons with ulcers!) Use in white sauces.

**Soy Bean** Use in many forms for high protein: soy sauce, soy beans, soy paste (called miso, obtainable in Oriental or health food stores, used in place of bouillon cubes, supplies proteins, vitamins, and minerals). Also fresh soy bean cakes (*tofu:* Oriental or health food stores) and sprouted soy beans.

**Miso Soup (soy) (per serving)** 1 tablespoon miso, 1 cup boiling water, 2 chopped scallions (or 1 small onion), pinch of sugar, 1 or 2 tablespoons wheat germ. Drop 1 beaten egg if desired. Cooks in 5 minutes.

**Four Basic Methods of Preparing Fish Fillets: Poaching.** Place fish in boiling "court bouillon"—1 cup dry white wine or dry vermouth, 1 cup broth, bay leaf, onion, parsley. After the fish is done and placed on platter, often the poaching liquid is boiled down to 1 cup or less which can be used in a cream sauce. Fish cooks in 6 to 10 minutes.

**Sautéing.** Make sure surface of fish is dry. Heat equal parts oil and butter in heavy frying pan. Gently fry fish. While first side is frying, sprinkle a bit of flour and some chopped parsley on the top to absorb juices. Turn only once. Total cooking time is 6 to 10 minutes depending on thickness of fish.

**Steaming.** There are special long, oval pots with a steaming basket inside. Without one, this method is impractical, and most Americans probably don't have one. Very fast: Place fish on perforated tray over boiling water. Cover. Remove to platter. Serve with lemon and parsley.

**Breading.** Dip slices in milk, then in bread crumbs. Fry in hot oil. Total time is 6 to 10 minutes.

# Index